DATE DUE			

Hate Groups

Revised Edition

Deborah Able

Enslow Publishers, Inc.

40 Industrial Road	PO Box 38
Box 398	Aldershot
Berkeley Heights, NJ 07922	Hants GU12 6BP
USA	UK

http://www.enslow.com

Library of Congress Cataloging-in-Publication Data

Able, Deborah.
    Hate groups / Deborah Able.—rev. ed
       p. cm. — (Issues in focus)
    Includes bibliographical references (p. 103) and index.
    Summary: Examines the historical roots of modern American hate crimes, some of the people and groups that carry out such crimes, and what their motivations might be.
    ISBN 0-7660-1245-X
    1. Racism—United States—Juvenile literature. 2. United States—Race relations—Juvenile literature. 3. White supremacy movements—United States—Juvenile literature. 4. Antisemitism—United States—Juvenile literature. 5. Hate—Social aspects—United States—Juvenile literature. [1. Hate crimes. 2. Hate groups. 3. Race relations. 4. Prejudice.] I. Title. II. Series: Issues in focus (Hillside, N.J.)
E184.A1A23   2000
305.8'00973—dc20
                              99-041174
                                 CIP

Printed in the United States of America

10 9 8 7 6 5 4 3 2

To Our Readers: All Internet addresses in this book were active and appropriate when we went to press. Any comments or suggestions can be sent by e-mail to Comments@enslow.com or to the address on the back cover.

Illustration Credits: AP/World Wide Photos, pp. 8, 90; Library of Congress, pp. 11, 23, 24, 27, 33, 37; National Organization for Women, p. 100; Pat Rocco/International Gay and Lesbian Archives, p. 78; Southern Poverty Law Center, pp. 43, 97; University of Idaho/College of Law/Jerry Prout, p. 64; U.S. Attorney General's Office, p. 58; Web site, p. 17; The White House, p. 92.

Cover Illustration: Matt Rainey/The Star-Ledger.

Contents

A Rising Tide
of Hatred

On June 18, 1984, a radio talk-show host, Alan Berg, stepped from his car in front of his apartment in Denver, Colorado, his arms full of groceries. Within seconds he was dead, killed by bullets from an illegal automatic weapon wielded by members of a white supremacy group who hated Berg because he was Jewish.

—

On November 12, 1988, three young men in Portland, Oregon, encountered three other young men. The first three were white; the other three were Ethiopian. Before their confrontation ended, Kenneth Mieske, Kyle Brewster, and Steven Strasser had murdered

5

one of the Ethiopians, Mulageta Seraw, by beating him repeatedly on the head with a baseball bat.

—

On August 23, 1989, Yusuf Hawkins went to Bensonhurst, a community in Brooklyn, New York, to answer an advertisement for a used car. He was surrounded by a group of young men from the predominantly Italian-American neighborhood who were wielding baseball bats. Within minutes, Hawkins was mortally wounded by a gunshot. Hawkins was African American; his killers were white.

—

On August 19, 1991, Yankel Rosenbaum, a Jewish scholar who was visiting relatives in Brooklyn, was murdered by a gang of African-American men angered by the death of an African-American youngster killed accidentally by a car whose driver was Jewish.

—

On New Year's Day, 1993, an African-American man, Christopher Wilson, was set on fire. He was burned over more than 40 percent of his body. His attackers, Mark A. Kohut and Charles P. Rourk, were white. They left a message near his body signed "KKK."

—

On July 15, 1993, FBI agents arrested eight people accused of plotting to bomb the First African Methodist Episcopal Church, assassinate Rodney King and other prominent African-American figures, and ignite a race war throughout Los Angeles. All eight of the people arrested were white.

—

On November 8, 1995, Eddy Wu, an Asian American,

was carrying groceries to a car when he was viciously stabbed and left for dead by Robert Page. Earlier that day Page had decided to "kill me a Chinaman . . . [because] they got all the good jobs."[1]

—

In the summer of 1996 a bomb exploded at Olympic Stadium in Atlanta, Georgia, killing two people and injuring more than one hundred others. The alleged bomber, Eric Rudolph, follows the teachings of the Identity Church movement, which claims that the white race and the United States are superior to all other races and nations. The Olympics emphasizes building a world in which all races and nations are equal.

—

On November 18, 1997, Oumar Dia, a West African immigrant, was waiting at a bus stop in Denver, Colorado, when Jeremiah Barnum and Nathan Thill, two white men, shot and killed him. The murderers were members of a skinhead organization that espouses white supremacy. At Barnum's trial in 1999, the court concluded that the men murdered Oumar Dia because he was African American.

—

On February 15, 1998, in Fort Worth, Texas, Robert Neville, Jr., and Michael Hall kidnapped Amy Robinson, age nineteen, whom they falsely thought was African American. They used her for target practice and killed her. Said one of the murderers, "It was supposed to be a racial thing. . . . We picked up a couple of guns and were going to go out and shoot black folks."[2]

On June 7, 1998, James Byrd, Jr., was beaten, chained to a truck and dragged three miles to his death along a highway outside Jasper, Texas. His attackers were white; Byrd was African American. At the trial of the first man, John William King, it was revealed that during the attack King had referred to The Turner Diaries, *an infamous white supremacy book.*

John William King, front, and Lawrence Russell Brewer were escorted from the Jasper County Jail on Tuesday, June 9, 1998, in Jasper, Texas. King and Brewer were sentenced to death, and Shawn Allen Berry was sentenced to life in prison for the murder of James Byrd, Jr.

On October 7, 1998, in Laramie, Wyoming, Russell A. Henderson and Aaron J. McKinney robbed and brutally beat Matthew Shepard, a gay college student. After the attack, they tied Mr. Shepard to a fence in subfreezing weather. He died five days later. The attackers allegedly targeted their victim because he was gay.

—

On the Fourth of July weekend, 1999, in Indiana and Illinois, Benjamin Smith, a fervent devotee of the World Church of the Creator, which advocates Aryan supremacy, went on a killing spree. He shot eleven people—Asian Americans, African Americans, and Jews—killing two of them before he killed himself. Smith was twenty-one years old.

—

On August 10, 1999, Buford U. Furrow, Jr., shot five people—four of them children—at a Jewish day care center in Los Angeles because he was "concerned about the decline of the white race and he wanted to send a message to America by killing Jews."[3] Furrow also shot and killed a postal carrier because he was not white.

The Many Forms of Hate

Different people, different years, different places, but all of the horrible incidents listed above have one thing in common: The attackers hated the people who were their victims because in some way those people were different from them. In some cases the difference was racial, in some cases the difference was religious, in one case the difference was sexual orientation, and in some cases the differences were a combination of factors. But because these crimes were based on people's intense dislike of people who are different from them, they fall into a category that law enforcement officials call hate crimes.

The Federal Bureau of Investigation (FBI) reported a rising incidence of hate crimes in the United States during the first half of the 1990s. This is particularly ironic and disappointing because the United States, more than any other nation on earth, is made up of people of all colors, religions, and ethnic backgrounds. Many of the first European settlers came here to escape religious persecution. Our laws are designed to protect all people equally. The Statue of Liberty has stood in New York's harbor since the 1880s to welcome strangers to a land that promises equal political and economic opportunity. Wave after wave of immigrants—from Europe, from Africa, from Central and South America, from Asia—have come to the United States to escape the kind of racial and religious persecution that not only exists in, but is often protected and even perpetrated by, the governments of many other countries.

Since World War II, America's commitment to civil liberties for all has grown even stronger. The civil rights movement of the 1950s and 1960s brought African Americans the rights that had been guaranteed them under the United States Constitution but that had been denied them in practice. Borrowing the tactics that had worked for the civil rights movement, women, Hispanics, and homosexuals have all worked with great success for greater equality in society.

Because of this democratic tradition of tolerance

In the late nineteenth century, thousands of immigrants entered the United States through New York's harbor. The Statue of Liberty, standing at the entrance of the new land, symbolized the promise of protection from the religious and ethnic discrimination they had faced in their homelands.

for all, hate crimes appear even more horrible than other acts of violence. Not only do the attackers hurt and sometimes kill other people, they assault the basic principles of democracy upon which our country was founded.

To combat hate crimes, it is necessary to understand the nature of these crimes and the people who commit them. Although most hate crimes are individual acts, many hate groups that condemn others because of their race or beliefs exist in America. The members of these hate groups are responsible for a relatively small portion of the hate crimes, but they are responsible for spreading hatred that may encourage others to commit these kinds of crimes. When a person is troubled, mentally unbalanced, or lacking in self-confidence, he may listen to the words of a hate group and turn those words into violent action.

In some countries, hate groups would simply not be allowed to operate. However, a basic premise of American democracy is freedom of speech. Even when people say hurtful things with which others do not agree, their right to say them is protected by the United States Constitution. Many people who would never join a hate group and who do not believe the things that hate groups say defend the right of hate group members to write and say what they believe. A basic reason for free speech is that if it is denied to one group, it can later be denied to other groups. Defenders of free speech believe that the best way to contradict speech that is hateful and usually untrue is by open, truthful speech. Censorship, they believe, is not effective in fighting hate groups; more effective is education about tolerance and diversity. Such programs provide information about hate groups and refute the content of their propaganda.

Concerned about the rising number of hate crimes, in 1993, the federal government passed a law requiring the FBI to compile statistics from local and state police about the numbers of hate crimes committed each year. In 1997, the most recent year for which federal statistics were available, the FBI found that in forty-five states there had been over eight thousand hate crimes (or bias crimes, as they are sometimes called, because the attackers demonstrate their bias—or prejudice—against their victims). An analysis of these crimes showed that 60 percent of the assaults were based on race, another 17 percent on religion, 13 percent on sexual orientation, and 10 percent on ethnic background.[4]

By recording hate crimes, law enforcement officials have also been able to draw several conclusions about them. First, hate crimes tend to be extremely brutal. Because the attacker has no respect for the victim as a person of equal status in the society, he feels no remorse in destroying or ending the person's life. Second, unlike most other crimes, hate crimes tend to be focused on strangers. In other words, the attacker rarely knows his or her victim before committing the crime. For African Americans, Jewish Americans, recent immigrants, or homosexual Americans, who are the leading victims of hate crimes, this means that any stranger is a potential attacker. Third, hate crimes are often committed by people in groups. Most violent crimes—75 percent, in fact—are carried out by individuals. However, over 60 percent of hate crimes are committed by groups of people, which demonstrates the importance and power of groups in the world of hate crimes.

Hatred Based on Stereotypes

Hate crimes are based on stereotypes—generalized, oversimplified, or exaggerated ideas—that one group of people holds about another group of people. Creating negative images about a group of people enables the hate group to justify its attacks. For example, hate groups believe many negative stereotypes about Jews, such as that Jews control the media and the banking industry in America, that Jews are more loyal to Israel than they are to the United States, and that Jews are greedy and aggressive. Hate groups stereotype African Americans as lazy, lacking in intelligence, violent, overly sexual, and eager to live off welfare instead of working for a living. Homosexuals are often characterized by hate groups as sexually promiscuous people who spread the AIDS virus throughout the world.

If a person is willing to believe that every Jewish person is a threat to the United States because Jewish people control the media, or that all African Americans are subhuman in intelligence, or that homosexuals are responsible for AIDS, then it is easy for that person to justify beating up or even murdering such a person. This violence is illegal and is condemned by most Americans, who believe that prejudice is wrong and anti-American. The members of most hate groups are white males who believe they represent true Americans, despite the overwhelming sentiment against their beliefs. Most of the members of these hate groups define themselves as true Christians. However, nearly all of the organized Christian religions have denounced the violent actions of people whose violence puts them very much at odds with the peaceful and tolerant messages that mainstream churches preach.

Some members of hate groups can be called *neo-Nazis*, a term that means "new Nazis," referring to their adherence to the philosophy and practices of Adolf Hitler, who led Germany during the 1930s and 1940s. Hitler and the original Nazis preached hatred against Jews, homosexuals, and gypsies, among others. In what became known as the Holocaust, Hitler and his followers killed and imprisoned millions of people before they were defeated by the United States, Great Britain, France, Russia, and the other Allied nations during World War II.

The anger expressed by neo-Nazis and other kinds of hate groups has been triggered since the 1960s by such programs as affirmative action and social welfare programs designed to help the poorer members of American society, who are often African American, Hispanic, or recent immigrants. As the federal and state governments have become increasingly committed to providing equal opportunities for all Americans—especially African Americans, Hispanics, and women, who have historically been oppressed—some of the white males who once dominated the economy feel threatened.

As certain groups have received attention from the government, their public identities as separate groups have also become more noticeable. Modeling themselves on the Black Pride movement of the 1960s, different groups have chosen to separate and proclaim their differences as a way of gaining the attention necessary to assert their place in society. Hispanic Pride, Gay Power, and various groups within the women's movement have promoted their groups by capturing the attention of the public with their slogans, demonstrations, and organizations.

Freedom of Speech and the Language of Hate

As the actions of these groups have become front-page news, the groups have also become the subject of the entertainment media. Until very recently in our nation, radio, movie, and television censorship prohibited the use of even the mildest swearwords on the air or onscreen. Since the late 1970s, however, rock groups and moviemakers have become more and more outrageous in their use of racial and ethnic slang words of the type that are used by the members of hate groups. These entertainers maintain that they are either joking or simply saying in song or through movies what people are saying privately. People who are concerned about the amount of violence in today's entertainment world maintain that "hatred has become an integral part of American mass culture, finding expression in its art, music, politics and humor."[5]

Whether the expression of hatred in rock music is seen as freedom of expression or merely an attempt to shock and sell records, it is undeniable that there is increasing use of racial epithets and violent imagery in the lyrics of current rock music. In the early 1990s, rappers such as Ice-T, 2 Live Crew, and N.W.A. routinely sang about violence against women and gays and justified the use of racial slurs on the grounds that they were African Americans themselves. One hit song of the group N.W.A. was based on the hero blasting his girlfriend with an assault rifle. In "Watcha' Looking At?" Audio Two sang of a man who looks gay and for that reason deserves to be punched. The heavy metal group Guns N' Roses sold 4 million copies of their album *G N'R Lies*, which contains lyrics that most critics consider to be antiblack, anti-gay and anti-immigrant. In 1991, Ice Cube's album *Death Certificate* included songs that called for burning down stores owned by Koreans and for the murder of a man because he was Jewish. A New Jersey rock group called Dying Breed sings anti-Semitic songs as fans shout "Sieg Heil!" and give the Nazi salute.[6] All of these groups used lyrics that were derogatory toward many groups of people.

This symbol of white supremacy was found on one of the many Web sites that express a message of hate.

The rap groups of the 1990s were generally composed of minority musicians who justified their music by claiming to bring hatred into the open. Other hate music, such as skinhead music, is more direct and has seemingly no positive reason for its existence. Although they have a small following, music groups that call themselves the Pro-White Alternative advertise on the Internet and claim they are the music of Resistance. For example, in their album *Crush the Weak*, the group Berserkr sings songs filled with antiblack and anti-Jewish lyrics. In *Swindler's List*, they claim that the Holocaust never happened. Other groups, such as Nordic Thunder, Skrewdriver and the New Minority sing songs with similar messages of hate. Many of these groups, such as Dirlewanger and S.S. Totenkopf, have German roots. They celebrate in music Hitler's legacy of hate and intolerance. For some young people, it may be difficult to separate the messages in the different forms of music, particularly when the words are often the same.

Musicians are not the only entertainers who use hatred in their messages. Many comedians have made ethnic jokes, gay jokes, and jokes about women the basis of their acts. Female comics also joke about men. Howard Stern, one of the most popular radio announcers in the country today, regularly entertains his audience by using African Americans, Jews, Hispanics, gays, women, and the disabled as targets for his brand of humor. Stern has been very successful and has moved his commentary from radio to books to a movie, *Private Parts*, released in 1998.

In the United States, all performers are protected by the constitutional guarantee of freedom of speech. Although the Federal Communications Commission, which regulates the media, has tried at times to limit the excessive language of people like Stern, these attempts have been generally unsuccessful. Most Americans support freedom of speech, and even those who are upset by the violence in the language of mass media entertainers disagree about its impact. Many social historians maintain that music groups and entertainers merely mirror the society in which they are found. They do not create violence; they simply reflect the violence around them.

For whatever reason, many observers believe that violence based on hatred is on the rise in the United States and elsewhere. How to prevent its further growth and how to reduce the tensions among racial groups, between men and women, and between homosexuals and heterosexuals is a leading challenge as Americans enter the twenty-first century. As is the case with so much in our society, the key to solving this problem is probably education. Too often schools are the sites of hate crimes, and the perpetrators of hate crimes are most often young people, especially young men.

Learning about the groups who commit these crimes is the first step toward an educational solution to the violence they create. This book attempts to help with that first step.

2

The Roots of Modern American Hatred

In 1967, the African-American activist H. Rap Brown, who was critical of Martin Luther King, Jr.'s, peaceful attempts to bring about the civil rights revolution, claimed, "Violence is as American as cherry pie."[1] What Brown meant was that throughout the history of the United States, from the time that the first Europeans set foot on this continent five hundred years ago, people have attempted to take land or run governments by excluding other people through a variety of methods, including violence. The United States was founded on the principles of freedom, democracy, and tolerance for all.

For each of these noble principles, however, there has been a dark side. The grim shadow of democracy has been the majority's control over minorities; the shadow of freedom has been the freedom to hate and to say hurtful things about others; and the shadow of tolerance has been prejudice against each new group that enters the society.

In 1991, two researchers, Michael and Judy Ann Newton, cataloged thousands of acts of violence based on race or religion that had occurred in North America over the past five hundred years.[2] This violence followed the same pattern as more recent hate crimes: It can be defined as "harmful or destructive action consciously directed against an individual or group because of race or creed."[3]

From the beginning, the continent of North America promised new economic opportunities for immigrants. For the earliest Europeans, the Vikings, this meant fresh fishing grounds. For the Spanish, new opportunity meant gold and land. For the dominant colonial group, the English, economic opportunity meant land and trade. The Vikings had a history of killing those in their way; they had virtually wiped out the Skrellings, the native inhabitants on Greenland, one of their first stops on the way to the New World. To the Spanish conquistadors, the American Indians were little more than wild animals. If the native people resisted the invaders, they were murdered. Not only did the English continue the Spanish destruction of the native population, but as soon as the English were established, they began to practice the religious and racial persecution that forms the roots of modern American prejudice.

Early Colonial Prejudice

The first English settlers to land in North America were loyal to the king and to the Church of England. These Virginians, as they would come to be called, were Anglicans who had little tolerance for the Puritans and Pilgrims who were settling in the area that is now Massachusetts. The Massachusetts settlers were nonconformists who did not follow the strict doctrines of the Church of England. Persecuted by the Church of England and the British government, they had no hope of full participation in the economic life in England. In large part, this is why they fled to the new continent.

It is not surprising that the Anglicans carried their religious prejudice with them. However, as soon as the nonconformists had established their colonies in New England, they, too, began to practice religious intolerance. Anyone who appeared to be different was subjected to persecution that ranged from banishment into the harsh wilderness to being burned at the stake. Hanging a woman in Salem for claiming to be able to hear God's voice directly without the intervention of a Puritan minister was an example of an early hate crime.

At the same time that the Northern colonists were practicing religious prejudice, their southern counterparts were introducing slavery. Beginning in 1619, the year that the first cargo of Africans was imported as slave labor for southern plantations, slavery was to create the most difficult social problem that the United States would face. By legally enslaving Africans, the early colonists created a legacy of second-class status for African Americans that serves as the background for today's racial hatred. Slaves were forbidden to share the family, education, work, and hope for a better future that formed the American dream for other immigrant groups.

Prejudice in the New Nation

By the time the Declaration of Independence was signed in 1776, the United States was well established

Slave owners in the American South beat the African Americans they held in bondage. Even after slavery was abolished, many still believed that African Americans were second-class citizens.

as a white, Protestant country. Slavery was fully entrenched in the South. A few people in the northern part of the nation considered slavery to be evil, but very few white Americans believed that African Americans should have equal political or social status with whites.

As the colonies formed constitutions, prejudice was legalized. The federal Constitution, the model for democracy in many ways, recognized slavery as an acceptable part of the new society through the Three-Fifths Compromise. Only 60 percent—or three fifths—of the slaves living in the South would be counted in determining the number of representatives a state could elect to the House of Representatives. In effect, African Americans did not count as full

The cruelest aspect of slavery may have been the separation of family members in slave auctions. Husbands were sold apart from wives, and children from their parents, because slaves were considered to be property, not people.

human beings. State constitutions written in North Carolina, Georgia, and New Jersey in 1776 forbade Roman Catholics to hold office, and the Vermont constitution, adopted the next year, stated that only Protestants could hold office.

As the new nation got under way in the early nineteenth century, religious prejudice continued to be the main force behind hate crimes. The white Protestant men in power in the early 1800s appeared to have forgotten that their ancestors had once been immigrants. New waves of immigrants faced hostility that was frequently based on their religion. (As long as slavery was legal, there was no reason to worry about African immigrants sharing in the economic prosperity of the nation.)

Between the 1820s and the 1850s, a "nativist" movement swept through the country. Based on the assumption that white Protestants were the true Americans, this movement was responsible for hundreds of acts of violence, directed most often against Roman Catholics. Before this time, the number of Catholics in the country had been so small as to pose no threat to the Protestant majority. A sharp increase in immigration from Roman Catholic Ireland, particularly in the cities of the Northeast, appeared to threaten the majority, even though as a total percentage of the population, Roman Catholics at that time would never exceed 15 percent.

In the 1820s, gangs of boys in New York and Boston beat up nuns and priests in the name of the nativist movement. In 1834, the largest nuns' residence in Boston, the Mount Benedict Convent, was burned to the ground. That same year, the inventor of the telegraph, Samuel F. B. Morse, warned in a letter to a New York newspaper of "A Foreign Conspiracy Against the Liberties of the United States." Morse wrote that the Pope's "henchmen" were entering the country as immigrants and planned "to establish a Romish kingdom in the Mississippi valley."[4] When the Pope sent a block of marble to be included in the construction of the Washington Monument, a gang stole it and threw it in the Potomac River.

By the 1840s, the situation had worsened. The nativist movement had become the basis for a conservative political party, the American Party. Also known as the Know-Nothing Party because of the secrecy practiced by its members, this group received a good deal of support, especially in local urban elections. The potato famine in Ireland from 1845 to 1848 caused immigration from that nation to increase. In 1845, one hundred thousand people, most of them Roman Catholic, emigrated from Ireland to the United States. The platform of the American Party included these planks: No Catholic should hold any political office; no foreign-born Protestant should hold any political office; and people should have to wait twenty-one years before applying for United States citizenship.

The Civil War and After

The nativist movement reached its peak in the 1856 election. In the presidential race, former president Millard Fillmore ran on the American Party ticket and won one fifth of the vote. The Know-Nothings

The American—or "Know-Nothing"—Party gained strength in the 1840s as more and more immigrants entered the United States. Committed to a white Protestant ruling class, the Know-Nothings printed posters such as this, which represented their picture of an ideal American.

were successful in local elections in New York, Massachusetts, Rhode Island, New Hampshire, Connecticut, Pennsylvania, Delaware, Maryland, and California. Although only 7 percent of the population in 1856 could be classified as immigrants, the popularity of the American Party demonstrated what a powerful force prejudice could be in American politics. Nearly one hundred fifty years later, Pat Buchanan and other extremely conservative politicians would use nativist language when they appealed to voters to elect them. For example, David Duke, an avowed white supremacist politician, promised voters that their children will never live in "an America where alien cultures and values will dominate."[5]

The nativist movement waned as the nation faced civil war. Violence and oppression had been constant factors in the lives of African Americans since their arrival on this continent. Africans were captured by Englishmen and Spaniards and forced in chains to endure a horrible ocean voyage to the New World; any act of resistance was met with beatings and often death. Throughout the two hundred fifty years of slavery, violence against African Americans was condoned as a necessary part of keeping these people in bondage. Slave overseers were allowed to punish slaves physically—whippings were routine, and rebellious slaves were often beaten to death. Slavery, like hate crimes, is part of the history of racism and discrimination in the United States. After all, the only difference between a person who was allowed to be enslaved and one who was not allowed to be enslaved was the color of his or her skin—or even an ancestor's skin color. In many Southern states, having a great-great-great grandparent of African heritage classified a person as black and thus subject to enslavement.

With the end of the Civil War, white Americans, who made up the majority of the country's citizens and who controlled the government completely, had to deal with the fact that the 4 million ex-slaves were now entitled by law to be citizens of the United States. Before the war, the South, and much of the North, had assumed that African Americans would never be full citizens, that white people were superior to black people, and that the two races would never mix. It had been illegal in southern states to teach slaves to read and write. Slaves were not allowed to vote, to serve on juries, to have money of their own, to own property, or even to marry. Slaves did not even control their own families; their white owners could sell part of a family at any time to a plantation far away, where the person would never see his or her loved ones again. These laws and customs reinforced the idea that African Americans were inferior to whites.

The Fourteenth and Fifteenth Amendments to the Constitution gave African-American males the same political rights as white males. For many white Americans, sharing the political and economic life of the nation equally with freed slaves was unacceptable. They decided that the best way to prevent African-American citizens from exercising their new rights was to carry out a campaign of violence against them. This violence against African Americans has remained an ugly fact of life in America. From the post–Civil War lynchings in the South to the bombing of African-American churches during the civil rights movement to the murder of James Byrd, Jr., in 1998, African Americans have faced more violent prejudice in America than any other group.

Organized Hatred—the Ku Klux Klan

The idea of intimidating African Americans through violent means gave rise to one of the most infamous hate groups in American history, the Ku Klux Klan (KKK). Although the original Klan was formed by a band of former Confederates and operated solely in the South, the Klan expanded in the twentieth century and now operates throughout the United States. Klansmen dressed in white sheets who burn crosses on hillsides or on the front lawns of the homes of African Americans typify hate groups for many Americans.

The original Klan was organized in Pulaski, Tennessee, by a small group of former Confederate soldiers. These young men were extremely embittered by their loss in the Civil War. In addition to the humiliation that all soldiers feel when they lose, these Southerners felt that their whole world had been turned upside down. Virtually all of the war had been fought on Southern soil, and the property damage to the South was estimated at $10 billion. The emotional toll on white Southerners was also great because their society was in danger of being totally rearranged. African Americans, who had been at the bottom of the social ladder, were now being given freedom, land, and the promise of education and full participation in Southern politics and economic life. Not only that, they were being protected by enemy Yankee soldiers.

In the beginning, the Klan was planned as a fraternity of white Christian Southern men who would get together for social reasons. It was not until 1867 that the idea really took hold and membership grew. In that year, a former Confederate general, Nathan Bedford Forrest, became the Grand Wizard of the Ku Klux Klan. Forrest was a superb horseman, and his nickname was the horse wizard; his title in the Klan was derived from that nickname. Under Forrest's leadership, the Klan was transformed into an organization of terror. These Klansmen wore sheets to hide their identities and to appear more terrifying in the night. They hoped that poorly educated, superstitious African Americans would think they were ghosts when they appeared. Their scare tactics went well beyond costumes, however. They burned homes and black schools, whipped African-American men who tried to vote, and lynched (illegally hanged) African-American men whom they thought had touched—or even spoken to—white women. Wherever the Klan appeared, they burned a cross as a symbol of white supremacy.

By the early 1870s, the Klan had been so effective in terrorizing Southern African Americans that almost none voted. Conservative white southerners recaptured control of southern state governments and legalized the segregation of African-American people. In the late 1800s, laws were passed throughout the South and in some northern states prohibiting African-American people from using the same public facilities as white people, from riding on the same train cars as white people, from eating in the same restaurants as white people, from serving on juries, and even from being buried in the same cemeteries as white people. Any time that an African American was even suspected of violating one of these laws, Klansmen donned their sheets and went after the alleged offender. African Americans were often lynched. By most government estimates, during the years between the birth of the KKK and the end of World War I, there were more than five thousand lynchings in the South.

By the early twentieth century, life for African-American Southerners was grim. They realized that they had no future in the South because they could never fully participate in politics or the economic system. When World War I brought the opportunity for work in the factories of the North, African Americans moved out of the South by the thousands. The Ku Klux Klan, also enticed by the prospect of jobs, moved with them.

With the end of World War I, the KKK boomed because its members added two new groups as their targets: Jews and Roman Catholics. William Simmons, an Atlanta businessman, became the leader, or Grand Wizard, of the modern Klan. He hired two public relations experts, Edward Y. Clarke and Elizabeth Tyler, to help him recruit new members to the Klan. Seizing on Americans' disillusionment with the war, Clarke and Tyler promoted the idea that American soldiers had died because of a war that had been created by a conspiracy of international Jewish bankers and Eastern European immigrants who were either Jewish or Roman Catholic. The Klan's new motto was "100 percent Americanism." Klan leaders defined 100 percent Americanism as *100 percent Protestant* and 100 percent white. To emphasize his beliefs, William Simmons liked to pull out his weapons in front of an audience, lay them on a table in front of him and

William Simmons, first head of the modern Ku Klux Klan, opposed equal rights for African Americans, Jews, and Roman Catholics. He gained many followers for his "100 percent Americanism" in the 1920s.

announce, "Now let the Niggers, Catholics, Jews and all others who disdain my Imperial Wizardry come on."[6] By the end of the 1920s, the Klan had 4 million members.

World War II and International Hatred

During the 1930s and 1940s, Klan membership declined as Americans dealt with the crises of the Depression and world war. During World War II, Adolf Hitler led Germany. Hitler's party, the National Socialist Party, was known as the Nazi Party. Although Americans always opposed the Nazi plans to conquer Europe, they eventually learned of other Nazi plans that were so horrible that many people regard Hitler and his followers as the most evil people in modern history. Hitler claimed that all of Germany's problems were the fault of the Jews living in Germany and other parts of Europe. He developed a plan known as the Final Solution that called for the imprisonment or murder of all Jews living in Germany and in any lands that the Nazis captured. Hitler's special forces, the SS, rounded up Jews, robbed them of all their possessions, and separated parents from their children. The Jews were placed in special prisons, called concentration camps, where those who were able to work were forced to do so, and those who were considered unfit for labor—for example, old people and children—were gassed to death. Although the Jews were Hitler's primary target, his troops treated gypsies and homosexuals the same way. When the war ended and the concentration camps were liberated by Allied soldiers, the world learned the extent of Hitler's hatred and madness. The murder of 11 million people, including 6 million European Jews, has come to be called the Holocaust. (Denying that the Holocaust ever existed is a favorite theme of the most extreme anti-Jewish hate groups.)

The horrors of the Holocaust prompted many Americans to examine their own prejudices, particularly anti-Semitism. However, many Americans continued to condone prejudice against African Americans, who, in spite of making many strides toward equality during the war, were still very much second-class citizens. With prejudice came hatred and brutality.

Civil Rights—Progress and Reaction

The next wave of violence against African Americans came with the civil rights movement of the 1950s and 1960s. As African Americans gained the support of many white Americans in their quest for equality, the minority of Americans who continued to hate African Americans on account of race became increasingly violent. On September 15, 1963, four African-American girls were killed when their church in Birmingham, Alabama, was bombed. A member of the Tennessee KKK, J. B. Stoner, was implicated in the crime. Quite a few civil rights workers, both African American and white, including Martin Luther King, Jr., were beaten, shot, and murdered in other ways throughout this period. Ironically, this era also brought about the greatest gains in political and economic equality for African Americans and for other minorities, since the Civil War. Often this would prove to be the pattern for hate crimes. Great gains in a group's civil rights are frequently followed by renewed violence against the group.

For example, Asian Americans, whose numbers are increasing in the United States, have been victims of violence since the late nineteenth century when people from Japan and China began emigrating to the West Coast in significant numbers. After the Civil War, immigrants from China, seeking work in the mines and railroads, clustered in California. Almost from the beginning, they were met with violence. In 1871, a white mob burned the homes and stores of Chinese living in Los Angeles and murdered at least twenty Chinese people in the process. In 1882, the federal government joined in the hostility against Chinese immigrants by excluding any more Chinese from entering the United States.

Although the laws against Chinese immigration were eventually rescinded, violence against Asian Americans continued. During the early twentieth century, the Japanese were the targets of hatred and violence. Anti-Japanese feelings culminated in the imprisonment, during World War II, of thousands of Japanese Americans in internment camps on the West Coast. Most of the people who were imprisoned were American citizens; many of them had been born in the United States. Solely on the basis of their ethnic identity, they were accused of being threats to the United States because we were at war with their ancestral country.

At the beginning of World War II, the United States government ordered all Japanese Americans living on the West Coast to be rounded up and placed in internment camps. These people lost their property and jobs solely because of their ethnic identity.

Since World War II, many other Asian Americans have faced violence and discrimination. In 1989, Jim Loo, a Chinese American living in North Carolina, was murdered by two white men who erroneously believed that he was Vietnamese and who blamed him for the deaths of American soldiers in the Vietnam War. American soldiers during the Vietnam War routinely used racial epithets to describe both their South Vietnamese allies and their North Vietnamese enemies. They carried this prejudice home with them when they were discharged. At the end of the 1980s, many Americans endorsed the advertising campaign undertaken by the Detroit automobile industry, which blamed Japanese car makers for slow business and unemployment among American car workers. The idea that Asians, both here and in their homelands, were taking jobs from Americans led to the 1995 attack on Eddy Wu described in Chapter 1. It is also the kind of thinking that, in 1989, led Patrick Purdy to open fire with an automatic weapon on a school yard in a predominantly Asian neighborhood in Stockton, California, killing five children and wounding thirty others. Purdy explained his crime by saying, "The damn Hindus and boat people own everything."[7]

Thus, modern-day immigrants from Asia have joined the ranks of Americans who have been victims of hate crimes. From the Irish and Eastern European Jews of the nineteenth century to the Asians and Hispanics of the twentieth century, immigrants to America have found not only the welcoming beacon of the Statue of Liberty but also violence and hostility. Since the late twentieth century, another group of people, homosexuals, has joined the roster of those whose lives and property are endangered by hate groups.

Since the 1970s, homosexuals have become more visible in American society. As has been true for other groups in the United States, the more visible and more accepted they have become, the more susceptible they have become to hatred and violence. In 1969, the New York City police raided the Stonewall Inn, a bar in Greenwich Village that catered to gay customers. Prior to this raid, gays had greeted such raids without resistance. On this night, however, they fought back. After "Stonewall," which became a symbol of gay pride and gay activism, homosexuals won greater acceptance and greater civil rights. The AIDS epidemic, which mushroomed in the 1980s, united gay rights activists even more because a high percentage of the victims of this disease were gay men. Conversely, attacks against gays increased because hate groups publicized the belief that gay men were responsible for the spread of AIDS throughout the population. The National Gay and Lesbian Task Force, a gay activist organization, began compiling statistics on violence against gay men and women. Between 1988 and 1991, they found that acts of violence against gays increased 161 percent in Boston, Chicago, New York, Minneapolis/St. Paul, and San Francisco, cities where the gay population is highly visible. In 1997 alone, more than fourteen hundred Americans were the victims of crimes in large part because they were—or were suspected of being—gay.[8]

The inclusion of gays on the list of targets for hate groups has clearly accelerated the violence against them. Gays have joined African Americans, Jews, and Asian Americans as victims of hate-group rhetoric and action. In the past, many gay Americans were able to avoid detection because, unlike African Americans and Jews, they were able to keep their identities as homosexuals secret. As gays come out of the closet— that is, openly express their homosexuality—they are more prone to attack by those who hate them.

3

Hate Groups

Although most hate crimes are not committed by people who belong to organized hate groups, organized hate groups are extremely important in understanding the hate crimes that are committed. Because these groups are well organized, they are able to influence a great number of people. Hate groups hold meetings to recruit new members and to publicize their feelings.

Hate groups often communicate with their members through newsletters. During the last decade, they have become increasingly sophisticated about using modern technology to communicate. Hate groups use computer networks, public access television stations, and even video games to get their messages across to their supporters. These methods are very effective. In fact, the Internet has provided hate groups with a way to reach people whom they could never before reach. The Internet may, in fact, be responsible for a new surge in hate group activity. Many observers who follow the activities of hate groups estimate that the number of people who formally belong to hate groups probably represents only 10 percent of the total number of people who read the literature published by the groups, log on to their Web sites, and share their beliefs.

When an unaffiliated person or group of people commits a hate crime, no one knows whether they were influenced by pamphlets or a television program written by or sponsored by an organized hate group. However, understanding the philosophy and programs of the major hate groups in the United States is one way to begin to understand the thinking of people who commit violent crimes that are motivated by hatred.

The Ku Klux Klan

The oldest and best-known hate group in America is the Ku Klux Klan. For more than 135 years, the Ku Klux Klan (KKK) has adhered to the white-supremacy beliefs of its founders, who supported the Confederacy during the Civil War. It has continued the use of strange names and the practice of secret rituals that began with Nathan Bedford Forrest. Today members of the Klan are given a booklet, the Kloran, that explains the philosophy and rules of the Klan so that new members will understand the traditions of the group. Each local area is organized as a den with a Cyclops as its leader. The Cyclops is assisted by twelve Terrors and two Nighthawks. Local dens are organized as Provinces, and the Provinces are joined as Realms. The Realms are headed by Grand Dragons, and the whole organization is under the control of the Grand Wizard.

Although the names sound as if they are from a fantasy novel, the KKK is anything but fiction. One woman, who has left the Klan and regrets ever having joined, recalled that at weekly meetings of her den, she helped teach the "lesson of the day."[1] One such lesson involved a situation in which an African-American child had been injured in a car accident. The Klan members gathered for the "lesson" were asked whether they would use mouth-to-mouth resuscitation to save the child's life. The correct answer, which they had to shout in unison, was no. At parades and weekend gatherings, Klansmen and Klanswomen demonstrate against Jews, African Americans, Asians, homosexuals, and Hispanics.

By the 1980s, there were three major Klan leaders and three major branches of the organization. In spite of its significant membership (estimated at one hundred thousand in the mid-1990s), many people thought that the Ku Klux Klan no longer existed, partly because it is split into many factions. However, the emergence of David Duke as a national political figure convinced most Americans that the

Although many Americans like to think that the Ku Klux Klan is part of the country's past, the modern Klan is very active in some areas of the nation.

Klan—or at least Klan thinking—is still a powerful force. Duke had been the Grand Wizard of the Klan from the mid-1970s until 1980. By the middle of the 1980s, he had renounced his Klan membership, calling it a "youthful mistake,"[2] but he ran for the Louisiana state legislature in 1989 on a platform that sounded ominously like the white supremacy of the KKK.

The founder of a white supremacist organization called the National Association for the Advancement of White People, Duke published a newsletter explaining his views. They mirror the philosophy of the KKK. He wrote:

> Immigration along with nonwhite births will make white people a minority totally vulnerable to the political, social, and economic will of blacks, Mexicans, Puerto Ricans, and Orientals. A social upheaval is now beginning to occur that will be the funeral dirge of the America we love. I shudder to contemplate the future under nonwhite occupation; rapes, murders, robberies multiplied a hundred fold, illiteracy such as in Haiti, medicine such as in Mexico, and tyranny such as in Togoland.[3]

Duke was elected to the Louisiana state legislature. Then in 1990 he decided to use the same racist platform to make a bid for the governorship of that state. What Duke told the Louisiana voters was that the white citizens of Louisiana and of the United States in general had lost their political and economic power because of affirmative action and government spending on aid for teenage mothers and other forms of welfare payments. Duke implied that the people who benefited from government programs were always African Americans, Hispanics, or immigrants.

The majority of Louisiana's white voters were persuaded by what he had to say—but that was not enough to make him governor. In the late 1990s Duke ran again, making a bid for a congressional seat from a heavily Republican parish in Louisiana. In his campaign speeches, he referred to the themes in his autobiography, *My Awakening*. In this book Duke espouses many antiblack, anti-Jewish, and also anti-government opinions. He describes racial equality in the twenty-first century as "the modern scientific equivalent of believing that the earth is flat."[4] Duke has also been able to capture new followers by using the Internet. His Web site, which provides a forum for his ideas, a marketplace for his book, and an opportunity for him to highlight government activities that he finds objectionable, is linked to other Web sites that share his agenda. Some of these, in turn, are linked to the Ku Klux Klan.

Just as Duke has a Web site explaining his position, so, too, do the various splinter groups of the Ku Klux Klan. The Knights of the Ku Klux Klan, which claims to be the most numerous branch of the organization, has a site promoting its vision of America as a "white Christian civilization." Another Klan site connects to more radical white supremacist groups. Yet a third, the Knights of the White Kamellia, has a site that regularly publicizes issues that concern this chapter of the Klan. In 1999 a typical Klan concern was the suspension of Josh Letney, a high school student in Jasper, Texas, the town where James Byrd, Jr., was dragged to his death. Letney was suspended for wearing a Confederate flag belt buckle. His high school felt that Letney's choice of apparel was insensitive and racist, since the Confederate flag was the symbol of a nation that favored African-American slavery and Byrd's death was racially motivated. The Kamellia believe that wearing the belt buckle symbolizes Josh's right to free speech. They also argue that his suspension provides further proof that white Americans are under attack.

An important aspect of Klan membership is belief

in a narrow version of Christianity. Although the vast majority of American Christians stress love and tolerance for all as basic tenets of their religion, some hate groups distort Christianity to exclude others, not include them.

Identity Christians

Although Identity Christians do not have a central church organization as do Baptists or Presbyterians or Methodists, for example, they share a common ideology. The Anti-Defamation League (ADL), a Jewish civil rights organization, has called their beliefs the glue that binds the different hate groups operating in America today. The ADL is particularly wary of Identity followers because strong anti-Semitic feelings are at the heart of their preaching. Identity churches have sprung up all over the United States since the movement was founded in 1946 by Wesley Swift, a Grand Wizard of the KKK. Identity believers maintain that the "chosen people" were the white Europeans and Englishmen who settled in North America. They call these people Aryans. They also believe that all Jews are descendants of a union between Adam and Eve's evil son, Cain, and the snake in the Garden of Eden. They believe that Jews are satanic people who conspire at all times to overthrow white Christians. Anyone who is not Jewish or Aryan is one of the "mud people," people who are on a spiritual level with animals and have no souls.

Identity Christians rewrite history with Jews as the villains. A typical Identity pamphlet, written by David Lane, one of the men convicted of conspiring to kill radio host Alan Berg, included this interpretation of American history:

> At the time the Jews took over our monetary system via the Federal Reserve, and instituted the income tax in 1913, the White race constituted about 40 percent of the Earth's population. Since then, the Jews have instigated two World Wars and fomented the Russian Revolution. These three events alone resulted in the death of over 80 million white Christians, most of them being young males and the genetic cream of our race.
>
> Next they laid such heavy taxes on the White workers of the world that it became, if not impossible, very financially impractical to have children. At the same time, the Jews took the taxes from the labor of productive Whites and gave it to non-Whites, both here and abroad, encouraging them to have from ten to twenty children. They used their media to insult and emasculate the White man while depicting non-White males to be heroes so White women would desert their race by the millions. The result is that the percentage of child-bearing women in the world today who are White and married to White men is at best 4 percent.[5]

Nobody knows how many Identity adherents there are in the United States, but there are certainly more than fifty Identity congregations. The most famous—or infamous—of the Identity churches, however, is Richard Butler's Church of Jesus Christ Christian in Hayden Lake, Idaho. Butler's church is affiliated with Aryan Nations, a paramilitary hate group that Butler heads. In an interview with a *Newsweek* reporter, Butler explained his beliefs:

When the Declaration of Independence talks about "one people," it's not talking about a nation made for Asia, Africa, India [or] the Soviet Union. That's a document based on a Christian people. We have watched like frightened sheep as do-gooders sniveling about the underprivileged gleefully grabbed our children by the nape of the neck and rubbed their faces in filth to create equality.[6]

Butler's Identity Church, like various Ku Klux Klan groups, has a Web site and a newsletter. Among the themes of the newsletter, *The New World Today*, is the message that the United States government is an evil, racist (antiwhite) organization. Butler and his followers view the United States government as having fallen into the hands of a corrupt and wealthy Jewish conspiracy. In the April 1998 issue, Butler wrote, "Jews control the wealth of the world and in turn control the governments."[7]

Another "church" dedicated to preaching messages of hatred is the World Church of the Creator (WCOTC). The invention of Ben Klassen (an immigrant from the Ukraine), the World Church was formed in 1973. Like Butler's church, the World Church views Jews, African Americans, and other minorities as the enemy. Unlike Butler's church, however, the World Church is anti-Christian. The World Church has a creative Web site that includes a colorful, engaging page for children. The Web site urges the church's followers to "gird for total war against the Jews and the rest of the . . . mud races of the world."[8] Calling for a racial holy war, which they have given the acronym RAHOWA, the World Church claimed three thousand members in the 1990s.

During the 1990s, their campaign suffered from a serious setback with a successful lawsuit from the Southern Poverty Law Center. In March 1994, the World Church of the Creator was found guilty of inciting two members of their group to murder Harold Mansfield, Jr., an African-American Gulf War veteran, and was ordered to pay a large settlement to Mansfield's survivors. Nevertheless, the WCOTC continues to recruit members who sometimes turn to violence. In July 1999, Benjamin Smith, a fervent WCOTC supporter, embarked on a killing spree in Illinois and Indiana. He shot eleven people—Asian Americans, African Americans and Jews—killing two of them before he killed himself. Matthew Hale, head of the WCOTC, claimed that he did not condone Smith's violence, but he expressed no concern for the victims. Smith had been named Creator of the Year by Hale and the WCOTC.

Members of the WCOTC and Identity followers maintain that they have a right to their beliefs under the freedom of religion provision of the First Amendment. Most, like Hale, condemn violent acts. Because of their race war message, however, they may contribute to violence. Other groups that voice racist philosophy openly call for violence.

The National Alliance

After George Wallace ran unsuccessfully for president in 1968 on a racist platform, some of his supporters founded the National Youth Alliance. In 1970 William Pierce, a former officer of the American Nazi Party and a physics professor, took over the organization and in 1974 dropped Youth from its title. In 1978, Pierce published a novel, *The Turner Diaries*, which has influenced a number of violent racists, including Oklahoma City bomber Timothy McVeigh. *The Turner Diaries* tells the story of a race war financed by a small guerrilla band through robberies and assassinations. The reason for the race war is the takeover of the world by a Jewish international conspiracy under whose tyranny whites are forced to intermarry with African Americans and Asians and government loans are given to mixed couples who live in white neighborhoods. A group of white super-patriots under the leadership of the hero, Turner, overthrows the Jewish government, destroys Israel with nuclear weapons, and creates a white Christian paradise.

The book is still in print, and thousands of copies are sold annually. It is now available in bookstores and online. Pierce's fantasy is not limited to this book. Pierce also penned the novel *Hunter*, dedicated to Joseph Paul Franklin, a man on death row for bombing a series of synagogues and killing eighteen people. In the dedication Pierce writes that Franklin "was the Lone Hunter, who saw his duty as a white man and did what a responsible son of his race must do." Pierce also has a Web site and an Internet radio broadcast each week called American Dissident Voices. In part because of his successful use of the Internet to get his message across and to recruit new members, the National Alliance has been dubbed by the ADL as "the single most dangerous organized hate group in the world today."[9] They estimate that the Alliance has at least one thousand active members in twenty-six states.

The membership of the Alliance sets it apart from many other hate groups. Its followers tend to be older, better educated, and more anonymous. Often Alliance members do not even know each other's names. The Alliance purchased one hundred shares of AT&T stock in 1986 and tried to reverse the affirmative action policies of the company and to stop it from doing business with Israel. When an African-American sex offender returned to Traverse City, Michigan, in 1998 after serving his prison term, the Alliance drew attention to his presence and distributed flyers linking African Americans to the spread of AIDS.

While the National Alliance warns of the possible need for violence in the future to protect white civilization, it has not yet been convicted of any direct violence. Other groups, some of them influenced by Pierce's writings, have been convicted of violence.

The Order, the Posse Comitatus, and the Freemen

During the early to mid–1980s, a vicious group of men launched a series of terrorist attacks on the United States. Originally either members of the Ku Klux Klan or followers of Identity churches or the National Alliance, they were led by Robert Mathews, a zealot who died in 1984 after a shoot-out with federal authorities. His organization was called the Order.

The Order was described by one FBI agent as a "small cadre of individuals dedicated to violence [and] engaged in paramilitary activities."[10] Although small in number, they were described by the director of the FBI, William Webster, as "more dangerous than the Klan groups from which they emanated."[11]

In 1984, FBI agents searched the home of Gary Lee Yarbrough in Sandpoint, Idaho. They were looking for Yarbrough's brother. Yarbrough, however, shot at the agents, intensifying their interest in his house. When they gained entry, they found a shrine to Hitler and the gun that had been used to kill Alan Berg, the outspoken liberal radio commentator from Denver, Colorado. Berg was Jewish.

During the investigation, the FBI unraveled the history of the Order, which was also called the White American Bastion or the Silent Brotherhood. For at least three years, this group, under the direction of Mathews, had robbed and murdered in preparation for the creation of a "neo-Nazi homeland."[12] Mathews not only had read *The Turner Diaries*, but also had believed the book was a prophecy, not fiction. Mathews and his followers referred to the government of the United States as ZOG, the Zionist Occupied Government, a reflection of their belief that Jews (sometimes called Zionists because of their support of the state of Israel) had taken over America. They planned to overthrow the United States government. To do this, they needed money for arms and ammunition, and they planned to assassinate a few key Jewish people, among them Henry Kissinger, Norman Lear (a television producer), and Alan Berg.

Between 1983 and 1984, the Order managed to steal almost $4 million, most of it at gunpoint. Before each robbery, members of the group would join hands around one of their babies, who, according to them, represented the future of the Aryan race, and would chant, "From this time on I have no fear of death. I know that I have a secret duty to deliver our people from the Jew, the mud people and all who would dilute the Aryan race. One God, one race, one nation."[13]

After Berg's murder, members of the Order hid out throughout the Northwest, successfully evading law enforcement officials. One by one, however, they surrendered. The last holdout was their leader, Mathews, who refused to give himself up. In the end, he was trapped on Whidbey Island outside Seattle, Washington. After a gunfight with federal agents, the house where he was hiding caught on fire. He perished in the blaze in December 1984.

Mathews' last letter revealed the depth of his commitment to white supremacy. He wrote:

> The stronger my love for my people grew, the deeper became my hatred for those who would destroy my race, my heritage. . . . By the time my son had arrived, I realized that White America, indeed my entire race, was headed for oblivion unless white men rose and turned the tide. The more I came to love my son, the more I realized that unless things changed radically, by the time

he was my age, he would be a stranger in his own land, a blond-haired, blue-eyed Aryan in a country populated mainly by Mexicans, mulattoes, blacks and Asians.[14]

The Order's spree of violence ended with Mathews' death, but he has become a martyr to racists everywhere. His picture hangs next to Hitler's in Butler's church in Idaho. Butler holds an annual memorial service for Robert Mathews, and new men are constantly being recruited to carry on the battle.

The Order ended in 1984 when its members were arrested and sent to jail. However, in August 1999, Buford U. Furrow, Jr., a white supremacist with links to the Order, shot five people, four of them children, in a racially motivated attack on a Los Angeles Jewish community center. He also shot and killed a letter carrier, Joseph Ileto, because he was not white.

Furrow told a federal law enforcement officer that he fired at the day care center because "he was concerned about the decline of the white race and he wanted to send a message to America by killing Jews." [15] Furrow also was said to have had ties to the Identity movement.

A number of groups who share the Order's violent goals have since emerged. The Aryan Republican Army, which models itself on Mathews' group, is estimated to be responsible for more than twenty bank robberies and bombings between 1992 and 1996. In March 1998 the FBI uncovered a plot in East St. Louis, Missouri, to bomb the Southern Poverty Law Center, the ADL headquarters, and the

Simon Weisenthal Center in Los Angeles. Three men who claimed membership in The New Order were convicted of violating federal weapons laws.

While the Order was waging war against the government, the Posse Comitatus was also doing battle with the federal government for similar reasons. Founded in 1969 by Henry Lamont Beach, Posse members believe that the federal government is controlled by a Jewish conspiracy. The Posse is more of a movement than an organized group and has attracted adherents from Klan groups, Identity churches, and other anti-Semitic and racist groups. According to Elinor Langer, Terry Nichols, the alleged partner of Timothy McVeigh in the Oklahoma City bombing, "came straight out of the Posse Comitatus."[16]

Posse comitatus is Latin for "power of the county." Members of the Posse refuse to accept any authority higher than the county sheriff. Gordon Kahl, who became a Posse Comitatus legend, typifies the type of person who is attracted to the Posse. Kahl, a failed farmer, blamed his financial problems on income taxes and social security payments, which he believed had been foisted on American farmers by the evil forces that had taken over the federal government. He wrote, "These enemies of Christ have taken their Jewish Communist Manifesto and incorporated it into the Statutory Laws of our country and thrown our Constitution and our Christian Common Law (which is nothing other than the Laws of God as set forth in the Scriptures) into the garbage can."[17]

In 1983, two federal marshals in North Dakota

attempted to arrest Kahl for parole violations. He killed them. A decorated World War II veteran, Kahl holed up in a farmhouse in Smithville, Arkansas, and held off several lawmen, killing the local sheriff and wounding several others before he was killed. Kahl became a martyr to the cause for other hate group members. The image of the lone warrior holding off scores of federal agents reinforced the mission of those people who believe that their cause is not only just but divine. In 1996 in Jordan, Montana, this image recurred when federal agents battled with a small band of extremists called the Freemen. This group was related to the Posse Comitatus.

The Freemen held off the FBI in a siege that lasted more than eighty days. Like the members of the Posse, the Freemen hated the federal government and refused to pay income taxes or follow any other government procedures such as registering motor vehicles or following weapons regulations. The FBI wanted to arrest some of the Freemen on charges that ranged from mail fraud to armed robbery. They were eventually successful, but not before the media had beamed countless images of the Freemen, who saw themselves as heirs of the American frontier legacy of individualism and personal freedom, holding off the forces of the government. By the summer of 1998, four of the Freemen had been found guilty of a banking conspiracy; their leader was sentenced to eleven years in federal prison a few months later.

The FBI was particularly reluctant to engage the Freemen in a gun battle because of events in Waco, Texas, and Ruby Ridge, Idaho, in 1992. In both places small bands of extremists had violated federal regulations involving firearms. In both places the federal government determined that it was necessary to use violence to subdue the alleged criminals. And in both places deaths were linked to this decision.

In Waco, a small religious group called the Branch Davidians had established themselves in a private compound. Rumors of child abuse, arms stockpiles, and various other violations convinced Attorney General Janet Reno to give the go-ahead to an FBI plan to storm the compound and rescue the children and other people they believed were being held against their will. The plan backfired and the compound exploded from within, killing nearly all the Branch Davidians. Critics of the government action viewed the federal agents as having used far too much force to subdue a small band of citizens. This charge reinforced the view of the government as an evil power trying to wipe out dissenters. A 1999 investigation into the government's actions found that the FBI agents had miscalculated and that excessive force was ordered.

The Branch Davidians were not a white supremacy group, per se, but that same year the government laid siege to the property of an avowed white supremacist, Randy Weaver, in Ruby Ridge, Idaho. Weaver and his family lived in a remote cabin, and Weaver had been charged with arms violations. When he failed to show up in court, the FBI surrounded his property, determined to arrest him. In the ensuing struggle, Weaver's wife and young son were killed by FBI marksmen. Again, Turner's fiction

Attorney General Janet Reno gave the order that allowed the FBI to storm the compound of a small religious group called the Branch Davidians. The plan backfired when the compound exploded from within, killing nearly all the members of the religious group.

seemed to be coming true: The government was killing people whose only crime, in the extremists' eyes, was supporting white supremacy.

Influenced by events at Waco and Ruby Ridge, a devoted reader of *The Turner Diaries*, Timothy McVeigh, determined to take action against the federal government and begin the race war that Pierce had urged. McVeigh set a bomb that blew up the federal building in Oklahoma City, killing and wounding hundreds of people, including many children in a day care center. McVeigh was a loner who had been unhappy ever since his mother had left him and his father and siblings when he was quite young. Introduced to white supremacy writings while he was serving a stint in the army, McVeigh combined his army weapons training with his youthful fascination for guns and Pierce's call for a race war. It proved to be a deadly combination. While McVeigh has steadfastly denied that he is a racist, he admits that he shares Pierce's antagonism toward the federal government. McVeigh mailed clippings from *The Turner Diaries* to his sister just a few days before the bombing.

Skinheads

Incidents like the shoot-out at Ruby Ridge, the Oklahoma City bombing, and the standoff in Montana temporarily bring groups like the Posse or the Order into national attention and are upsetting to most Americans. Far more terrifying to many people because of their increasing visibility in American cities are the violent white-supremacist youths who join skinhead gangs. Skinheads not only act scary, they look scary. Their extreme haircuts and military garb, including combat boots, reinforce their violent image. They often wear the number 88 as shorthand for "Heil Hitler," because *h* is the eighth letter of the alphabet. Sometimes skinheads are members of organized hate groups, and other times they provide "security" for hate group events.

The association with Hitler reinforces the neo-Nazism popular with most skinheads.

The Skinhead movement began in England in the 1970s. Membership has spread throughout Europe and into the United States. The ADL, an organization committed to fighting anti-Semitism and violence against other minority groups, estimates that there are seventy thousand skinheads in thirty-three countries and six continents.[18] Germany is home to the single greatest number of skinheads, five thousand by a recent ADL estimate. In Germany and elsewhere, skinhead youths have developed their own underground culture. Skinheads listen to Oi! music, which advocates violence against nonwhites and Jews, and they play video games such as Aryan Test, where the object is to earn points by killing Jews.

There are conflicting reports about the numbers of skinheads in the United States, but the ADL estimates that their numbers remained relatively stable throughout the 1990s at about thirty-five hundred. In 1989, skinheads marched in the annual KKK parade in Pulaski, Tennessee, demonstrating their solidarity with older white supremacy groups. For the most part, however, the skinheads of the 1990s have remained unorganized. Their groups tend to be small and local and are found in areas as different as New York City and small towns in Utah. Bands of skinheads have colorful, expressive names such as the American Frontists, the Confederate Hammerskins, the Doc Marten Stompers, and the White Workers Union.

What skinheads have in common is their animosity toward Jews and other minorities and their willingness to use violence. American skinheads target racial minorities and immigrants. Skinheads everywhere have reacted violently to Jews and homosexuals. Other things that skinheads have in common are their race, age, and gender. For the most part, they are white males between the ages of thirteen and twenty-five. There are also some nonracist skinheads who wear the same look as skinheads but do not share their racist philosophy. Some of these skinheads are nonwhite. For example, there is a group called SHARP (Skinheads Against Racial Prejudice), which combats racial prejudice.

When the FBI uncovered a plan to start a race war in Los Angeles in the summer of 1993, it found that members of the group called the Fourth Reich Skinheads were in charge of the plot. The Fourth Reich Skinheads had been in existence for only two years, but in their court appearance on the charges of attempting to bomb the A.M.E. church and assassinate Cecil Murray, the African-American pastor of the church, members of the group admitted to other bombings, including a synagogue and the home of an African-American family. The ADL estimates that skinheads have been responsible for over twenty-five murders in the United States since 1990. In general, skinheads are not interested in political action. They advocate direct violence. When the police arrested a skinhead group responsible for murdering a man on Long Island in 1995, they found that the group owned a small arsenal that included assault weapons.

As the twenty-first century unfolds, some observers think that the Internet may provide skinheads with a way of attracting greater numbers by reaching out to more alienated young people. Young white males are the most common users of the Internet and the most likely candidates for skinhead membership.

White Aryan Resistance

One victim of skinhead violence was a young Ethiopian man, Mulageta Seraw. On November 12, 1988, he was walking with two companions on a street in Portland, Oregon. Three members of a skinhead group, East Side White Pride, attacked Seraw, beating him with a baseball bat and stomping him with their boots until they had crushed his head and killed him. Kenneth Mieske, Steven Strasser, and Kyle Brewster were found guilty of murder, and Mieske is serving a life term in jail. At his trial he explained that he killed Seraw because he was African American; after four years in prison, he still expressed no regrets about his actions.[19]

When he heard about the Seraw murder, Morris

Dees, a prominent civil rights lawyer and the founder of the Southern Poverty Law Center, felt that the members of East Side White Pride had not acted alone. The Southern Poverty Law Center joined with the Anti-Defamation League to prosecute Seraw's murderers. Dees acted as chief counsel. He believed that the young men had been recruited to kill by an older, better established hate group. He accused Tom Metzger, founder and head of White Aryan Resistance (W.A.R.), of sending agents from W.A.R. headquarters in San Diego to Portland to stir up the skinheads. Dees brought a civil case against Metzger on behalf of the Seraw family.

For two years investigators from the Southern Poverty Law Center worked at establishing a connection between W.A.R. and East Side White Pride. The ADL discovered that Dave Mazzella, an agent of White Aryan Resistance, had indeed been sent to Portland to recruit young white men to be soldiers in the hate war that Tom Metzger, his son, John, and their followers were advocating. Arguing that the Metzgers and their organization were responsible for inciting the skinhead youths in the murder of Mulageta Seraw, Dees brought a wrongful death suit on behalf of the Seraw family against the Metzgers and W.A.R. The jury agreed with Dees. Tom Metzger was forced to pay $5 million in damages and John Metzger $1 million, and W.A.R. was fined $3 million. Then Metzger appealed the judgment, which was one of the largest of its kind, but the appeals court upheld the original decision. In an angry response to the judgment, Tom Metzger used the kind of language

Morris Dees, a famous civil rights lawyer and the founder of the Southern Poverty Law Center, sued Tom Metzger and his organization, White Aryan Resistance. Dees argued that the group incited a group of skinheads to kill the Ethiopian Mulageta Seraw. The jury agreed.

which reinforced that the jury and Dees had been right in their estimate of his goals. He said, "We will put blood on the streets like you've never seen and advocate more violence than both world wars put together."[20]

Estimates of how many Americans support Tom Metzger and W.A.R. range widely. Certainly W.A.R. is one of the largest, most successful hate groups in the western United States. Although he is based in California, Metzger reaches a large number of people throughout the country via the Internet, a monthly tabloid, and a telephone hot line. Metzger, one of the first of the white supremacy group leaders to make use of the Internet, has done so very successfully. His site features crude cartoons and racist articles. Metzger repeatedly refers to white people as "nature's finest handiwork." Unlike many other white supremacist groups, he is not Christian. He is an atheist who frequently reminds his followers, "Your race and only your race must be your religion."[21]

Metzger takes full advantage of America's freedom of speech laws. Like many people who are anti-Semitic, he believes that Jews control the mass media in the United States, including film, television, and radio. For that reason, he welcomes new technology such as public access television and computer networks that challenge the limits of free speech. Under a 1964 federal law, public-access television channels must provide free time slots to anyone who wants them on a first-come, first-serve basis without censorship—although the law was modified in 1993 to prohibit "obscene materials, sexually explicit conduct or material promoting or soliciting unlawful conduct."[22]

Since 1984 Metzger's television show, *Race and Reason*, has broadcast his racist messages. Although several groups have tried without success to shut down Metzger's program because it advocates violence, *Race and Reason* has remained on the air. Metzger argues that he is simply stating an opinion. On a typical broadcast of *Race and Reason*, Metzger begins, "Hi, this is Tom Metzger . . . blazing a trail of real free speech, free speech for white working people for a change. *Race and Reason* is an island of free speech in a sea of managed and controlled news."[23] By grabbing onto the issue of free speech, Metzger attempts to justify his racist, anti-Semitic demagoguery as a legitimate expression of ideas.

W.A.R. is somewhat different from other hate groups. As Metzger explains it, "W.A.R. wears no uniform, carries no card, and takes no secret oaths; [it] doesn't require you to dress up and march around on a muddy street; [it] works the modern way, with thousands of friends doing their part on the job, behind the scenes, serving their race."[24]

In spite of the judgment against W.A.R. in the Seraw case, Metzger and his organization are going strong. Groups that monitor neo-Nazi behavior and hate groups consider W.A.R. and its Web site to be among the most virulent. It is certainly clear from Metzger's published writings that W.A.R. is a hard-line hate group.

In a campaign speech in 1992, Bill Clinton spoke out against "the voices of intolerance . . . that proclaim that some families aren't real families and some Americans aren't real Americans."[25] He could have been describing the messages of hate groups.

4

Why People Hate

Why do some people hate so much? What is there in the personalities of the members of hate groups that makes them hate people who are different from them? Why are they willing to commit violence—or at least condone it in others?

These questions have puzzled law enforcement officers, social workers, prison officials, clergy, and government officials. In fact, everyone who comes in contact with people who hate or who commit hate crimes tries to figure out what motivates the haters. Unfortunately, there are no easy answers to these questions. If there were, hate crimes could possibly be stopped. In the meantime, analysts try to look at the people who have committed hate crimes to see if there are any patterns in their lives.

Characteristics of Hate Group Members

Three of the most obvious similarities among hate group members are their age, their sex, and their race. Most of the members of hate groups are white males under age thirty.[1] Timothy McVeigh, the Oklahoma City bomber, fits this profile. Most of the people who commit violent crimes and are not formally associated with any organized hate group are also white males under age thirty.[2] The criminals currently serving time for the murder of Michael Griffith in Howard Beach, the murderers of Yusuf Hawkins in Bensonhurst, Vincent Chin's assailants in Detroit, the killers who conspired to murder Alan Berg in Denver, the attackers who shot and killed Jeremiah Barnum in Denver, the arsonists who burned Christopher Wilson in Miami, the plotters who await trial for their alleged plan to start a race war in Los Angeles—for the most part, these people were young, white, and male.

In his analysis of these haters, Morris Dees has called them "violent, angry, deeply troubled young men and a growing number of young women" and has concluded that "generally they come from deeply troubled, dysfunctional families and are fundamentally damaged long before they swing their first baseball bat at someone or plant their first pipe bomb."[3] Many of the young haters obviously do fit

Dees's and other sociologists' descriptions. For example, Greg Withrow, who, along with John Metzger, helped found the White Student Union on a number of college campuses around the United States, grew up in a house where he was verbally and physically abused by a violent, racist father. By the age of thirteen, he was homeless and living on the streets.[4]

Another hater who had a troubled childhood was David Lewis Rice, who on Christmas Eve, 1985, murdered Seattle attorney Charles Goldmark, his wife, and two sons because he believed that Goldmark was the "head Jew" and "top Commie" (Communist) of the Northwest. Rice also believed a theory found in some far-right hate literature that there were Communist Chinese poised in Canada and North Koreans lined up in Mexico ready to attack the United States. Rice's extreme paranoia was perhaps the result of a difficult childhood. His family had never shown him any love, and an accident as a child had left him scarred and blind in one eye, the target of countless jokes by his classmates. A loner because of his rejection by both his family and his classmates, Rice lived inside his head where his fantasies of persecution by other people grew to terrifying proportions and led him to his heinous final act.

Not all hate criminals are victims like Withrow and Rice, and not all people who grow up in troubled families commit hate crimes. In August 1993, when the plot to blow up the African Methodist Episcopal Church in Los Angeles (the largest, most influential African-American church in that city) was revealed, friends and neighbors of Christopher David Fisher, a twenty-year-old former Eagle Scout, were shocked to learn that he had confessed to have led the plot. Fisher had grown up in a stable, upper-middle-class home. His mother was a college professor and his father was an elementary school teacher. As an Eagle Scout, Fisher led a model life, encouraging other boys not to smoke or drink, but to participate in recycling and other environmental activities instead. Unlike Withrow, Fisher had not grown up in a house where racist language was common. But Fisher had joined the Fourth Reich Skinheads, an avowed hate group, and had quickly risen to a position of leadership within the group.

In addition to being young, white, and male, Timothy McVeigh was abandoned by his mother. Nevertheless, there is much about McVeigh that does not fit the profile of hate crime offenders. His neighbors described him as having a warm relationship with his father and sisters, his teachers complimented him on his good grades and school citizenship, and the family priest remarked upon his apparent religious devotion and concern for others. Though he was quiet and shy and liked to go off by himself with his .22-caliber rifle, McVeigh was not a troublemaker and was generally viewed as a polite, hardworking young man by the people in his small, western New York hometown.

The young white males who commit these crimes do not operate in a vacuum. They choose targets based on what they have heard at home, in school, or in the media. These crimes are no longer viewed as isolated actions. During their teenage years, all children wrestle with questions of identity. For those who are prone to prejudice, their search for self-esteem can lead them to put down—either verbally or physically—other people because of race, ethnic background, sexual orientation, or anything else that makes their identity different from that of the attacker.

Influences of Modern Culture

Youngsters who tend toward violence can find plenty of models for their actions. Although no one is absolutely sure about the impact of television on children, it is indisputable that American children watch a lot of television. By the age of sixteen, the average child may have watched hundreds of hours of television and seen thousands of acts of violence, including hundreds of murders. Shows such as *South Park* are very controversial. Its creators argue that by using racial epithets and portraying cartoon violence against handicapped or gay people, they are speaking out against hatred and prejudice. Their critics, on the other hand, contend that the show legitimizes the use of hate speech and violence toward people who are different. They maintain that name-calling and violence should never be humorous or entertaining.

There is one final explanation for why young men join hate groups: pure thrill. One observer of the rise of skinhead gangs in Germany has concluded that their growth has not resulted from the merger of the two halves of Germany, as unsettling as that has been, nor from poverty nor unemployment nor liberal permissiveness nor the breakdown of the family. Rather, he concludes that the young men in skinhead groups are "murderous punks" whose reward for terrorist acts is "not prison, but breathless TV coverage."[5] Other observers of Germany agree that the new skinheads are not the political storm troopers of Hitler's day who had a specific political agenda behind their hatred. Writes Jane Kramer:

> The skins say "Heil Hitler!" but they know nothing about Hitler, or the war, beyond the fact that Hitler exterminated people who were "different," which is what they like to do themselves. They do not even know about the "ethnic cleansing" going on a few hundred miles away in Bosnia now. They do not read newspapers. They read killer comic books and listen to Oi! music, which is a kind of heavy-metal rock about the pleasures of genocide. . . . They do not know that other people think of *oi* as a Yiddish word. They do not know Jews or anything about Jews, but Jews are certainly on their hit list, along with Turks, refugees and asylum seekers, anybody "foreign." . . . Most of them are not capable of— or interested in— explaining why they find foreign people or homeless people or handicapped people or any of the other people they kill unpleasant, or why they seem to enjoy killing those people. . . . They like to think of themselves as independent.[6]

Independent is one of the adjectives that is often used to describe Eric Rudolph, the fugitive who is accused of the Olympic Stadium bombing at the 1996 Atlanta games, a bombing at a gay bar in Atlanta, and the murder of a security guard in the bombing of an abortion clinic. It is believed that

Rudolph is living in the mountains of North Carolina, where he may be protected by people who "regard the fugitive as far less menacing than the federal and state agents sent to hunt him down."[7] By choosing to hide out in the mountains, Rudolph is identifying himself with the American tradition of the frontier—"that part that regards a man as a law unto himself."[8] While most of the people living in this area of North Carolina would not themselves take violent action against abortion clinics or gay bars, a majority share Rudolph's antigay, antiabortion views. In another time Rudolph might have been a swashbuckling pirate or a deerskin-clothed frontiersman, slaying enemies but earning heroic praise instead of condemnation for killing Indians, for example. In modern America, lack of respect for the government and for politicians means a lingering respect for "heroes" who take the law into their own hands, deciding who shall live and who shall die. In real life, this kind of thinking can lead to hate crimes.

Prejudice—the Root of Hatred

Whether hate crimes are committed by youths or older people, prejudice is at the root of the actions. Prejudice has been part of American society from the beginning, and it continues most often in neighborhoods where there is little contact with people who are different. When Yusuf Hawkins, a young African-American man, entered the community of Bensonhurst, New York, to look at a car that he had seen advertised, he was, for all intents and purposes, entering an alien territory. The vast majority of the people of Bensonhurst were white. The young men who attacked and killed Hawkins did not know many African-American people personally, and they were only too willing to assign racial stereotypes to the African-American stranger who suddenly appeared in their midst. They decided that he was there to date a white girl. It has long been part of the prejudicial myths about African-American men that they are a threat to white women. Without thinking through the validity of this stereotype, and certainly without asking Hawkins, the white teens simply acted violently, shooting the young man, killing him and ruining their own lives.

Myth and paranoia about nonwhite, Jewish, and Hispanic Americans is particularly strong in rural areas of the United States, especially in the West and Midwest. There is less contact in these areas with non-Christians and non-Caucasians, so there is less chance for an individual to have a friend or colleague of a different race or religion. The people in these rural areas do not see many African Americans, Hispanics, Jews, or Asian Americans, and most of their neighbors or relatives who are gay keep that fact well hidden or move to urban areas where they can live more openly. Throughout the twentieth century, hate groups flourished in these rural areas.

On October 23, 1984, Arthur Kirk, a Nebraska farmer, was killed in a shoot-out with a SWAT team of Nebraska state troopers. Kirk was bankrupt after a series of bad harvests, and as he brandished his M-16 in a futile attempt to keep his farm from being taken by the bank, he thought that the troopers were agents of Mossad, the Israeli Secret Service. The anti-Semitism reflected in Kirk's dying actions is perhaps the most deeply rooted of the hatreds felt by some white Americans in the rural Midwest and West.

Linking Prejudice and Poverty

Anti-Semitism is interwoven with the myth that the economy of the United States is controlled by international Jewish bankers. This myth is mentioned most often when times are bad in farm country, which has been the case since the mid-1970s. In a 1986 Harris poll taken in Nebraska and Iowa, the heart of farm country, nearly one third of the people polled agreed with the following statement: "Farmers have always been exploited by international Jewish bankers who are behind those who overcharge them for farm equipment or jack up the interest on their loans."[9] Nearly half of the population in both states agreed with this statement: "When it comes to choosing between people and money, Jews will choose money."[10] Even more damaging may be what James Coates calls "unexamined bigotry."[11] This is the casual use of hurtful, stereotypic language such as *jew down* (meaning "to drive a hard bargain") or *nigger in the woodpile* (meaning "to smell a rat"). The existence of this kind of unthinking prejudice among people who would never dream of committing a hate crime, argues Coates, "gives the haters a ready toehold."[12]

The 1980s were a devastating time for American farmers economically, but they were not the only group to have suffered. During the 1980s, the lower class in the United States grew larger and poorer. In 1977, one percent of the population was in control of 7 percent of the nation's income; by 1990 this same small group controlled 11 percent of the nation's income. While the 1990s have generally been regarded as a time of prosperity, it was not a good time economically for people on the lowest rungs of the socioeconomic ladder. Two people working full-time at minimum-wage jobs can provide less than 70 percent of the necessities for a family of four.[13] By the mid-1990s the proportion of Americans who were classified as poor had grown to nearly 25 percent. Americans in the lower and middle classes believed that their children were not likely to have a better life than theirs. As they see their share of the economic pie shrinking, some people look for villains to explain why this is happening to them. They turn to the stereotypic enemies that they have been taught are different and by their very differences are therefore evil.

Most Americans who harbor prejudices against one group or another are nonviolent. However, those who are violent hear the same messages. They learn "their culture and, as a result, [know] precisely those groups against which [they are] supposed to vent [their] anger."[14] Sometimes, tough economic times encourage violent reactions. When Vincent Chin was beaten to death in Detroit, his attackers made it clear that they blamed Chin—and other Asians—for the poor state of the American automobile industry. As they beat him, Ronald Ebens and Michael Nitz cried, "It's because of you we're out of work."[15] Thirteen years later the message was the same when Robert Page stabbed Eddy Wu because "they [Asians] got all the good jobs."

Visibility and Prejudice

Economic decline increases people's awareness of groups that they believe are competing with them for jobs and money. Increased visibility of minority groups can happen in other ways; it almost always leads to increased numbers of crimes targeted against their members. For example, the number of attacks on gays and lesbians has increased with their increased visibility in society. Dr. Howard Ehrlich, research director of a national institute that monitors prejudice and violence, has noted, "When a traditionally subordinate group becomes more visible, levels of conflict increase."[16] Gays had been nearly invisible to the majority of Americans prior to the 1970s. Since the revolution at the Stonewall Inn, gay Americans have become increasingly vocal about seeking equal civil rights with heterosexual Americans.

Other groups also suffer from surges in criminal attack when they are featured on the front pages. Holocaust services on college campuses are often followed by increased anti-Semitic graffiti, such as swastikas painted on the walls of Jewish student centers. The Persian Gulf War heightened Americans' awareness of the Arab population living in the United

Gay and lesbian Americans have become more visible as they have adopted the tactics of other groups in working for greater civil rights.

States and consequently led to attacks on them and their property. When American car dealers in Detroit sponsored a series of advertisements implying that the Japanese were responsible for the decline in American car sales, Japanese Americans who had nothing to do with the car industry found themselves under attack. In one of the most violent incidents, a Japanese-American realtor in California was killed.

Whatever their motives, people who hate lose their right to speak out against other people because of their different skin color or religion or ethnicity when their prejudice turns violent. Are crimes that are motivated by prejudice worse than other crimes? In recent years, more and more people have come to believe that criminal actions are deserving of greater punishment when they are motivated by prejudice.

5

Does Freedom of Speech Mean Freedom to Hate?

During the 1990s, many state and city governments attempted to reduce hate crimes by passing hate crime laws. These laws make a crime that is motivated by hatred based on the victim's race, religion, ethnic background, or sexual orientation a more serious crime than such an act would ordinarily be. For example, if a person burns down a store because the owner of the store is an Arab, the crime is considered to be more serious than if the criminal simply burned down the store as a random act of vandalism. The criminal who commits a hate crime has to pay a larger price for his crime—either pay a stiffer fine or serve a longer jail sentence.

Hate Crime Laws—Pro and Con

Some people believe that bias crime laws are unconstitutional. They believe that these laws violate the criminal's freedom of speech. If a person shouts "Kill the Jew" as he shoots at a Jewish person, should he pay a higher penalty than a person who shouts, "Kill that guy"? People who are committed to freedom of speech believe that laws making the person shouting the epithet pay a higher price may penalize people for their thoughts. The concern is that hate laws may violate freedom of speech by punishing how people think about other people.

The laws' supporters, on the other hand, argue that the enhanced penalties are necessary. They argue that hate crimes have a greater impact on victims than do other crimes. They also maintain that hate crimes have an impact on communities and not just the specific victims of the crimes. They believe that hate crime laws help police and courts take bias more seriously and help victims of such crimes have the courage to report them. Finally, they argue that hate crime laws do not abridge freedom of speech because they punish activities that are already defined as criminal. They point out that American criminal law has always weighed motivation in sentencing.

In the early 1980s, the ADL began to record a sharp increase in anti-Semitic incidents and crimes. At that point, the ADL proposed a law that could be adopted by the individual states. The bill had two primary components. First, the bill included an institutional-vandalism measure that was particularly important in anti-Semitic crimes. This part of the law "prohibited and provided increased penalties for vandalizing, defacing or damaging places of worship, cemeteries, schools or community centers."[1] The second section of the law was called the intimidation statute. Under this provision, there would be enhanced penalties (stiffer sentences) for crimes like harassment or assault if they were committed because of the victim's race, color, religion, national origin, or sexual orientation.

State and Federal Legislation

Over the course of the 1980s, every state except Nebraska, Utah, and Wyoming adopted some form of hate crime statute. Institutional-vandalism laws were the most commonly accepted, but twenty-nine states also introduced bias-motivated violence and intimidation laws. Some states, such as New Jersey, had enhancement laws. If a crime was bias-related, the criminal's punishment was moved up one degree. For example, a person found guilty of murder in the third degree faced the harsher penalty of second-degree murder if the crime could be proved to be motivated by bias. In 1990, the federal government passed the Hate Crime Statistics Act. Although this is not bias-crime legislation in the strict sense that the state laws are, the act is proof that the federal government as well as the state governments recognize the special nature of hate crimes. Some observers were surprised when President George Bush, a conservative Republican, signed this bill into law. The statute had been opposed in Congress for many years by other conservative politicians, especially Senator Jesse Helms of North Carolina, who objected to the inclusion of sexual orientation in the law. Many conservatives, like Helms, believe that including antigay crimes with other hate crimes legitimizes homosexuality as a way of life.

The law that President Bush signed simply requires the attorney general to keep statistical records on hate crimes. It does not change the way that hate crimes are prosecuted on the federal level. In approving the law, President Bush explained its purpose: "The faster we can find out about these hideous crimes, the faster we can track down the bigots who commit them."[2] But the law had its opponents.

Helms's concerns were not the only ones that were voiced. Collecting the information could be difficult and expensive. As terrible as hate crimes are, they make up a very small percentage of all crime in the United States. In 1997 the FBI reported eight thousand hate crimes, but there were 15 million crimes overall. James B. Jacobs and Kimberly Potter, legal scholars who have studied hate crime laws, have charged that the number of hate crimes is too small to warrant such attention.[3] With drug-related crime escalating, many law enforcement officials would rather concentrate on crimes that they believe hurt a greater number of people. Nevertheless, most people believe that hate crime laws are good and necessary. Forty states have passed bias laws.

Almost as soon as a state passes a bias law, it is tested in both state and federal courts. Courts are the place where the constitutionality of laws is tested, and it has been in the courts that hate crime laws have come up against the First Amendment to the United States Constitution, which forbids laws that "abridge freedom of speech."

Hate Crimes and the Courts

Late one night in June 1990, seventeen-year-old Robert Viktora, a white skinhead, snuck into the yard of the only African-American family living in a working-class neighborhood in St. Paul, Minnesota. Russ and Laura Jones were awakened by the flames that rose from the burning cross that Viktora had planted in their yard. The youth had purposely chosen the traditional Ku Klux Klan symbol used to threaten violence against African Americans.

The local police could have charged Viktora with trespass or disturbing the peace, but they chose instead to charge him under the hate crime law that both the city of St. Paul and the state of Minnesota had passed in the early 1980s. The city law made it illegal to place "on public or private property a symbol, object, appellation, characterization, or graffiti, including but not limited to, a burning cross or Nazi swastika, which one knows or has reasonable grounds to know arouses anger, alarm, or resentment in others on the basis of race, color, creed, or religion or gender."[4]

Viktora's lawyers and other defenders claimed that the law was unconstitutional. They argued that the language of the law was so broad that it interfered with the right to free speech. At his first trial, the judge agreed that Viktora was guilty of trespass and damage to another's property, but he also agreed with the defense attorneys that the hate crime law was unconstitutional. The case then went to the Minnesota Supreme Court.

The court disagreed with the first judge. According to the high court of Minnesota, Viktora's action was not protected by the First Amendment to the United States Constitution because the burning cross fell under the definition of "fighting words," which the United States Supreme Court in the case of *Chaplinsky* v. *New Hampshire* defined as "a direct tendency to cause acts of violence by the person to whom, individually, the remark is addressed."[5] Those who opposed the law pushed it to the United States Supreme Court, and on June 10, 1991, the Supreme Court agreed to hear the case, which was called *R.A.V.* v. *St. Paul* (Viktora's initials rather than his full name were used because he was a juvenile at the time of the crime).

A year later the Supreme Court rendered its decision against the St. Paul law. What the Supreme Court decided was similar to the decision of the first judge—they agreed with him that the law was too broad. By specifically mentioning certain forms of expression—the swastika or burning cross, for instance—the law, according to the Supreme Court, violated the free speech provisions of the First Amendment. Speaking for the majority of the justices on the Supreme Court, Justice Antonin Scalia argued that any law that limited forms of expression—such as the "fighting words" laws—had to be free of "content discrimination."[6] Many liberal-thinking people who do not usually agree with the conservative views of Justice Scalia agreed with him on this point. They argued that by singling out specific hateful words to be repressed, these words take on greater importance than they should. They also worried that content-based laws like the one in St. Paul could be expanded to "punish legitimate statements that upset people."[7]

In 1978 the United States Supreme Court had refused to hear the case of *Village of Skokie* v. *National Socialist Party of America*. In that case, a lower federal court had declared that neo-Nazis had the right to march down the street in a predominantly Jewish suburb. They held that the use of language or the expression of ideas that offends or upsets people is protected under the First Amendment. Their ruling stood. Clearly, the line between freedom of speech and "fighting words" is a fine one. Laura Jones, on whose lawn the cross was burned, said of Viktora, "He has the right to say anything he wants to, but he doesn't have a right to come up on our property and threaten us."[8]

Shortly after the Supreme Court's ruling on the Viktora case in Minnesota, the Wisconsin Supreme Court struck down Wisconsin's hate crime law. Once again the Village of Skokie case was elevated to the

United States Supreme Court. This time, however, the high court heard the case.

Wisconsin v. *Mitchell*, as the case was called when it was tried in the Supreme Court, began one night in October in Kenosha, Wisconsin. After seeing the movie *Mississippi Burning*, which was about the early years of the civil rights movement, Todd Mitchell, a young African American, encouraged a group of his friends to "move on some white people."[9] Gregory Riddick, a fourteen-year-old white boy, had the misfortune to walk by. Mitchell cried to his friends, "There's a white boy. Go get him."[10] The boys beat Riddick until he was unconscious, causing permanent brain damage.

Todd Mitchell was sentenced to two years in prison for the beating. In addition, he was sentenced to two more years under the terms of the Wisconsin law that called for sentence enhancement (that is, greater penalties) in the case of crimes where criminals "intentionally select"[11] their victims because of religion, race, ethnic origin, disability, or sexual orientation. It was the additional two years that Mitchell's attorneys protested. As in the Minnesota case, they argued that the hate crime law was unconstitutional. The United States Supreme Court, however, disagreed. Because the Wisconsin law targeted hate in general and did not refer specifically to any group, the Supreme Court found it constitutional. As Clarence Thomas, the only African-American Supreme Court justice, noted, the law could be used to try a group of African-American people who attacked another group of African-American people because they did not like their stand on civil rights.

Some people were concerned that the reason the Supreme Court upheld this law was that Mitchell was African American. Since the majority of hate crimes are committed by the majority—that is, white Americans—against members of minority groups, the Mitchell case was unusual. Those who are concerned about minority rights worried that this law could be used indiscriminately to increase the sentences of young African-American men who commit crimes against victims who just happen to be white.

Other state laws have been tested, both by state courts and by the Supreme Court. Ohio overturned its hate crime law in 1993; the court justified its action by saying that the law created "thought crime."[12] The Ohio case arose from an incident at a campsite when a white man, angry at an African-American camper's loud music, threatened him, using racial epithets. What would have been a misdemeanor was escalated to a crime carrying the punishment of an eighteen-month jail sentence under the provisions of Ohio's hate crime law. No violent action, other than shouting, had taken place, however, and the judge in the case ruled that the Ohio law punished the white man's thinking and was in direct conflict with his freedom of speech. This case, *State* v. *Wyant*, was appealed to the Supreme Court, which sent it back to the state for reconsideration. Reversing their earlier position, the Ohio court ruled that the law was constitutional, particularly in light of the Supreme Court's decision in *Wisconsin* v.

Mitchell. In the 1990s California and Oregon upheld their hate crime laws, and Delaware overturned its statute.

Federal Law

Proponents of hate crime laws are pushing for a federal hate crime bill that would apply to all the states equally. While a member of the House of Representatives, Congressman Charles E. Schumer of New York (who became a senator from that state) authored a bill that would direct the United States Sentencing Commission, the government agency responsible for setting the length of jail terms for federal crimes, to increase by three levels the sentence for anyone who is convicted of a crime that is "motivated by hatred, bias or prejudice, based on the [victim's] actual or perceived race, color, religion, national origin, ethnicity, gender or sexual orientation."[13] Although the bill passed the House of Representatives, it was tabled in the Senate, largely because of the efforts of North Carolina's senior senator, Jesse Helms, who was again concerned that this bill, like the Hate Crimes Statistics Act, might be construed as condoning homosexuality.

The 1998 murders of James Byrd, Jr., and Matthew Shepard gave new impetus to the passage of a federal hate crime bill. President Bill Clinton supports the passage of the Hate Crimes Prevention Act, which would expand federal law to include attacks based on gender, disability, and sexual orientation, as well as race, religion, and ethnicity. The

A stone cross was erected in March 1999 to mark the spot where Matthew Shepard was found lashed to a buck fence on the high plains east of Laramie, Wyoming. Shepard was allegedly targeted because he was gay.

new law, which is sponsored by Senator Edward Kennedy, a liberal Democrat from Massachusetts, would target all hate crimes, even when the defendant is not involved in a federally protected activity (e.g., voting, jury duty, attending school). President Clinton has said in support of the bill, "There is nothing more important to the future of this country than our standing together against intolerance, prejudice and violent bigotry."[14]

Other people oppose the bill on the same grounds that they have opposed similar state bills. They argue that the federal law would be unconstitutional because it gives some people's lives more value than others. As one critic wrote in opposition to the Washington, D.C., Bias-Related Crime Act of 1989, "The legislation in effect divides America into two classes: Those whose skulls can be cracked with a criminal penalty of, let us say, six months in jail, and those whose skulls are better protected by government and thus warrant nine months in jail if cracked."[15]

The inclusion of gender in the Schumer bill raises another interesting and controversial aspect of hate crime legislation. Should attacks on women, particularly rape, count as hate crimes? Is all rape, by its very nature, an attack based on gender? Several United States senators apparently thought so. Under the leadership of Senator Joseph Biden, its chief sponsor, the Violence Against Women Act passed through Congress in 1994. Title IV of the act provided that "crimes motivated by the victim's gender constitute bias crimes in violation of the victim's right to be free from discrimination on the basis of gender."[16] The Violence Against Women Act is not strictly a hate law because it does not call for enhanced penalties, but its supporters are motivated by their widely accepted belief that people who rape are demonstrating a deep hatred of women.

Once again, the bill's opponents are concerned that it violates the First Amendment because courts will be asked to judge what a person was thinking at the time of a crime. Some feminists are concerned because there may develop a distinction between a bad rape and a worse one (one motivated by hatred), and feminists have worked hard during the past

President Clinton speaking at an event in 1999 to promote the passage of the Hate Crimes Prevention Act, which would expand federal law to include attacks based on gender, disability, and sexual orientation.

decade to educate people about the horrors of all rapes, whether committed by a stranger in the night or a date on a college campus.

The passage of the Biden bill and the likely passage of the Schumer bill make one thing very clear. In the wake of increased attention to violence based on hatred, the United States has turned to the law to help end the hostility and crime. In a democracy, the majority must safeguard the rights of minorities. Usually that means protection from criminal actions, but it also means protection for unpopular views. In the case of hate crime legislation, these two goals may conflict.

6

Teenagers and Hate Groups

Hate groups can flourish only if they continue to recruit new members. In spite of schools' emphasis on tolerance, violence at high schools and on college campuses indicates that hate groups are having no trouble recruiting young people to their ranks. Many people think that the reason young people are willing to join hate groups in high school and in college is that they are uncertain about their own futures. Because they believe that the available portion of the American economic pie is shrinking, they are worried that other people will get a bigger slice. Some white males, especially, believe that African

Americans, Hispanics, women, and Asians should not take pieces of a pie that "belong" to them.

Often people believe that the young people who join hate groups are those with the least education and the least to hope for in the way of jobs. As a Berkeley, California, sociologist put it, "We used to assume that prejudice would go away when a more enlightened, higher-educated group of young people replaced a generation of bigots. That doesn't follow anymore."[1] Unfortunately, hate also flourishes on college campuses.

Hate on Campus

Consider these incidents, for example. In the fall of 1990, students at the University of Illinois surrounded a Jewish fraternity and shouted, "Hitler had the right idea."[2] At Brown University in Providence, Rhode Island, the campus was littered with anonymous pamphlets that read,

> Once upon a time Brown was a place where a white man could go to class without having to look at little African American faces, or little yellow faces, or little brown faces, except when he went to take his meals. Things have been going downhill since the kitchen help moved into the classroom. Keep white supremacy alive.[3]

At the University of Alaska, students sported T-shirts advertising their membership in the "Anti-fag Society," and at Syracuse University, students with similar ideas wore T-shirts advocating violence against homosexuals—"Club faggots, not seals." At the University of Wisconsin, a student told an Asian student, "It's people like you—that's the reason this country is screwed up. You don't belong here. Whites are always getting screwed by minorities and some day the Whites will take over."[4] At Yale University in 1997 antigay slogans were painted on the doors of students presumed to be gay.

On hundreds of college campuses in the 1980s, the response to the increase in racial and religious incidents was the development of campus speech codes. At Brown, at Wisconsin, at Michigan, and at Stanford, policies were instituted that punished students for using language that targeted other people because of race, religion, national origin, or sexual orientation. Many people, however, felt that these codes of conduct infringed on students' freedom of speech. They quoted Justice Oliver Wendell Holmes, who said,

> If there is any principle of the Constitution that more imperatively calls for attachment than any other, it is the principle of free thought—not free thought for those who agree with us but freedom for the thought we hate.[5]

Most campus speech codes, when tested in court, have been found to violate the First Amendment right of freedom of speech. As noble as the goal of the legislation may be, in practice it regulates student speech. The University of Wisconsin, Duke University, Indiana University, Brown University, and the University of Michigan have all had their speech codes challenged.

The Challenge of the Internet

The Internet has provided new challenges for the supporters of uncontrolled free speech. Millions of people, many of them teenagers, have discovered that the Internet is the single most efficient way to provide and gain access to information. Some hate groups, whose membership had not grown in years, have found that the Internet gives them the ability to recruit many new members. For example, the WCOTC increased its organization from thirteen to forty-one chapters between 1998 and 1999 through the creative use of a Web site designed to attract followers of all ages. There is even an interactive coloring book page filled with white supremacist symbols and a children's crossword puzzle with racist clues. Although *The New York Times* considers the WCOTC to be "perhaps the fastest-growing and one of the largest hate groups in the country," [6] it is certainly not alone. The various branches of the KKK are also using the Web to attract new members. The Klanwatch project of the Southern Poverty Law Center monitors twenty-nine separate Klan home pages on the Web and has found 127 active Klan groups operating in thirty-two states. This 74 percent increase in one year can be largely attributed to Web activity, according to the people monitoring Klan recruitment efforts.

Most people agree that parents have the right to monitor children's access to information, whether from the public library or television or the Internet. Most Internet companies have special software that

The members of the Ku Klux Klan are not only alive and well, but taking their children with them to rallies, to carry on the "cause" of white supremacy and racism.

allows adults to control what their children may access. However, as children get older, it becomes more difficult for parents and teachers to know what information they are receiving. Schools stress technological proficiency and urge teenagers to become familiar with computers and to use the Internet as a resource. What is not clear is how much influence hate groups will have over young people through their Internet messages. When tragedies occur, such as the school shooting in Littleton, Colorado, authorities are quick to examine the computer lives of the people involved in the crimes. Often, as in the case of the two boys in Littleton, there is evidence that they have been attracted to hatred and violence via the Internet. However, thousands of other young people may have logged on to the same sites with differing results. Very few are tempted to take violent action, and many may very well become upset with the message and vow to oppose the hatred that is expressed.

The Pain of Hatred

Although the legal system often provides a way for victims of hate crimes to defend themselves against their attackers, nothing protects the victims of hate crimes from the hurt and pain that bias crime brings—even when the crime is limited to hateful words. A Jewish girl who heard anti-Semitic remarks whispered about her in the hallway of her high school has said that she will never forget how bad she felt when she heard the hateful words directed at her because of her religion.[7] Her experience was not very different from that of eighteen-year-old Gordon Diefenbach, a gay teenager who eventually quit attending his Denver, Colorado, high school because of the physical and verbal attacks against him. Diefenbach remembers high school as a time of isolation: "If a teacher would have the class split up into groups, no one would want to be in my group. . . . Two years ago I tried to kill myself. I slit my wrists. . . . I didn't think I could go through life with everyone beating up on me, harassing me, hating me."[8] Diefenbach's experience was the same as that of anyone in a minority group who is victimized because of it. No matter how secure a person is, the sense of isolation, coupled with overt or implied violence because of the person's difference, is often more than a person can stand.

Being singled out for one's differences can be particularly painful during adolescence. In February 1994, a young woman named Revonda Bowen sat in an assembly at her high school in Wedowee, Alabama, and heard the principal announce that African-American girls or boys could not attend the prom with white boys or girls. She stood up and bravely asked the principal what she should do about the prom since her mother is African American and her father is white. The principal replied that her mother and father had "made a mistake, having a mixed-race child."[9] By expressing his belief that certain types of people are "mistakes," her principal was isolating Revonda from her classmates. The pain and embarrassment Revonda felt caused her to burst into tears. Shortly after the incident, the school board voted to suspend the principal, and Morris Dees of the Southern Poverty Law Center volunteered to prosecute Hulond Humphries, the principal, on Revonda's behalf. No matter how much protection the courts give her, however, Revonda will never be able to forget that moment in front of her entire high school when a person in authority said that she should never have been born because she was an example of race-mixing.

Violence against women remains a pressing issue. Members of the National Organization for Women, and their supporters, march to highlight the issue.

Educating Against Bias

Prohibiting hatred by limiting what people may say about other people appears to be unconstitutional. So, how should people who want to end hatred and violence go about it? The best way is more education. At several high schools in New York, a program dedicated to the memory of Yusuf Hawkins asks teenagers to talk openly about their prejudices. They are allowed to use the words that have been outlawed on some college campuses, but they must do so openly in a classroom where classmates who are African American or Jewish or gay can hear them.

Although the initial reaction is one of hurt and shock, by talking about their feelings and stereotypes, they reach a better understanding of one another. In a truly democratic society, schools have an ethical obligation to uphold freedom of speech. The best way to end hate speech is by showing with better words how harmful hatred can be.

Other school programs that are helping educate teenagers about the connections between hatred and violence are A World of Difference, sponsored by the Anti-Defamation League, and The Tolerance Project, originally sponsored by Barbara Jordan, the late congresswoman from Texas. Both programs have received national support from teachers' associations and school boards. Neither program shies away from the language of hate; instead, they help students examine the motivations behind such talk.

There are many organizations in the United States today that are committed to democracy and free speech and to ending hatred and violence. For more information, you can write to these groups, which are listed in "For More Information" on page 102. By discussing openly and honestly why we fear those who are different, we can stop hatred. When someone says something hateful about another person, it is not enough to say, "Shut up." We need to ask why that person feels that way. When we listen to song lyrics or comedians' jokes that put down other people, we need to ask why the artist has said this, and we need to consider whether we want to buy those records and repeat those jokes. Everyone thinking and working together can reverse the hatred.

For More Information

Groups that are concerned about hatred and hate groups in American society include the following:

Anti-Defamation League
823 United Nations Plaza
New York, NY 10017
<http://www.adl.org>

Hate Watch
<http://www.hatewatch.org>

National Gay and Lesbian Task Force
1517 U St., NW
Washington, DC 20009
<http://www.ngltf.org>

Southern Poverty Law Center
400 Washington Avenue
Montgomery, AL 36104
<http://www.splcenter.org>

Two programs that can be used in schools to teach about tolerance are:

A World of Difference
Anti-Defamation League
823 United Nations Plaza
New York, NY 10017

Teaching Tolerance
Southern Poverty Law Center
400 Washington Avenue
Montgomery, AL 36104

Chapter Notes

Chapter 1. A Rising Tide of Hatred

1. "Fighting Hate Across the Nation: Examples of Hate Crime Violence Against Asian Pacific Americans," n.d., <http://www.civilrights.org/lcef/hcpc/examples/asian.html> (March 15, 1999).

2. "Intelligence Project," n.d., <http://www.splcenter.org/intelligenceproject/lp-index.html> (March 15, 1999).

3. Frank Gibney, Jr., "The Kids Got in the Way," *Time,* August 23, 1999, p. 24.

4. "FBI Uniform Crime Reports, 1991–97," n.d., <http://www.fbi.gov/cr/crreports.html> (March 1, 1999).

5. Jack Levin and Jack McDevitt, *Hate Crimes: The Rising Tide of Bigotry and Bloodshed* (New York: Plenum Press, 1993), p. 33.

6. Andrew Gannon, "Racism Finds a Groove in Jersey Underground," *New Jersey Star-Ledger*, August 29, 1999, p. 1.

Chapter 2. The Roots of Modern American Hatred

1. H. Rap Brown, press conference in Chicago, 1967.

2. Michael and Judy Ann Newton, *Racial and Religious Violence in America: A Chronology* (New York: Garland Publishers, 1991), p. ix.

3. Ibid.

4. James Coates, *Armed and Dangerous: The Rise of the Survivalist Right* (New York: Hill and Wang, 1987), p. 23.

5. David Duke, "America at the Crossroads," n.d., <http://www.davidduke.com/writings/crossroads.html> (March 1, 1999).

6. Coates, p. 33.

7. Jack Levin and Jack McDevitt, *Hate Crimes: The Rising Tide of Bigotry and Bloodshed* (New York: Plenum Press, 1993), p. 96.

8. "FBI Uniform Crime Reports, 1991–97," n.d., <http://www.fbi.gov/cr/crreports.html> March 1, 1999).

Chapter 3. Hate Groups

1. Claire Safran, "Our Life in the Ku Klux Klan," *Good Housekeeping,* June 1992, p. 139.

2. Elinor Langer, "The American Neo-Nazi Movement Today," *The Nation,* July 16–23, 1990, p. 95.

3. David Duke, "My Awakening," n.d., <http://www.christian-aryannations.com> (February 15, 1999).

4. Ibid.

5. Quoted in James Coates, *Armed and Dangerous: The Rise of the Survivalist Right* (New York: Hill and Wang, 1987), p. 23.

6. Mark Starr, "Violence on the Right," *Newsweek,* March 4, 1985, p. 25.

7. Edward Butler, "Editorial," *The New World Today*, April 1998.

8. "RAHOWA! This Planet Is All Ours," n.d., <http://www.creator.org/frames.html> (February 15, 1999).

9. "Explosion of Hate: The Growing Danger of the National Alliance," n.d., <http://www.adl.org/explosion_of_hate/front_introduction.html> (February 15, 1999).

10. Starr, p. 23.

11. Ted Gest, "Sudden Rise of Hate Groups Spurs Federal Crackdown," *U.S. News and World Report,* May 6, 1985, p. 68.

12. Coates, p. 57.

13. Ibid., p. 58.

14. Ibid., p. 52.

15. Frank Gibney, Jr., "The Kids Got in the Way," *Time,* August 23, 1999, p. 24.

16. James Ridgeway, "Terry Nichols's Posse," *The Village Voice*, October 7, 1997 <http://www.villagevoice.com> (February 15, 1999).

17. Coates, p. 104.

18. "A.D.L. to 4 Countries Recently Hit by Skinhead Violence," n.d., <http://www.adl.org/frames/front_ search.html> (February 15, 1999).

19. Lauren Tarshis, "Brotherhood of Bigots," *Scholastic Update,* April 3, 1992, p. 2.

20. Jack Levin and Jack McDevitt, *Hate Crimes: The Rising Tide of Bigotry and Bloodshed* (New York: Plenum Press, 1993), p. 103.

21. Tom Metzger, "Religion," <http://www.resist.com/ Religion.html>(February 15, 1999).

22. Joseph Berger, "Forum for Bigotry? Fringe Groups on TV," *The New York Times,* May 23, 1993, p. 34.

23. Langer, p. 85.

24. Ibid., p. 89.

25. "Fugitive Surrenders after Idaho Siege," *Facts on File,* September 17, 1992, p. 686.

Chapter 4. Why People Hate

1. Morris Dees, "Young, Gullible and Taught to Hate," *The New York Times* (August 25, 1993), p. 32.

2. Helen Zia, "Women in Hate Groups," *MS,* March/April, 1991, pp. 20–27.

3. Dees, p. 32.

4. Michelle Green, "Trouble," *People,* September 21, 1987, p. 43.

5. Josef Joffe, "Why 1992 Is Different from 1932," *U.S. News and World Report,* December 14, 1992, p. 33.

6. Jane Kramer, "Neo-Nazis: A Chaos in the Head," *The New Yorker,* June 14, 1993, pp. 52–55.

7. Tony Horwitz, "Run, Rudolph, Run," *The New Yorker,* March 15, 1999, p. 46.

8. L. J. Davis, "Ballad of an American Terrorist," *Harper's Magazine,* July 1986, p. 53.

9. James Coates, *Armed and Dangerous: The Rise of the Survivalist Right* (New York: Hill and Wang, 1987), p. 197.

10. Ibid., p. 198.

11. Ibid., p. 262.

12. Ibid.

13. John E. Schwarz, "The Hidden Side of the Clinton Economy," *The Atlantic Monthly,* October 1998, p. 21.

14. Jack Levin and Jack McDevitt, *Hate Crimes: The Rising Tide of Bigotry and Bloodshed* (New York: Plenum Press, 1993), p. 48.

15. Ibid., p. 58.

16. George M. Anderson, "People Are Getting Hurt," *Commonwealth,* February 26, 1993, p. 16.

Chapter 5. Does Freedom of Speech Mean Freedom to Hate?

1. Kenneth Jost, "Hate Crimes," *CQ Researcher,* January 8, 1993, p. 12.

2. Ibid., p. 14.

3. James B. Jacobs and Kimberly Potter, *Hate Crimes: Criminal Law and Identity Politics* (New York: Oxford University Press, 1998), p. 57.

4. "Breaking the Codes," *The New Republic,* July 8, 1991, p. 12.

5. Jost, p. 14.

6. Ibid.

7. "Breaking the Codes," p. 8.

8. Ibid.

9. "Bad Motives," *The New Yorker,* June 21, 1993, p. 4.

10. Ibid.

11. Jeff Rosen, "Bad Thoughts," *The New Republic,* July 5, 1993, p. 4.

12. Jost, p. 15.

13. Ibid., p. 16.

14. Rebecca Leung, "Attacking Hate," July 8, 1998, <http://www.ABCNEWS.com> (November 23, 1999).

15. John Leo, "The Politics of Hate," *U.S. News and World Report,* October 9, 1989, p. 24.

16. Pub. Law No. 102–322, 108 Stat. 1796, tit. IV (Sept. 13, 1994).

Chapter 6. Teenagers and Hate Groups

1. Art Levine, "America's Youthful Bigots," *U.S. News and World Report,* May 7, 1990, p. 59.

2. Ibid.

3. Pete Hamill, "Black and White at Brown," *Esquire,* April 1990, pp. 67–68.

4. Jacobs and Potter, p. 119.

5. *United States* v. *Schwimmer*, 279 U.S. 644, 654–655 (1929).

6. Michel Marriott, "Rising Tide: Sites Born of Hatred," *The New York Times,* March 18, 1999, p. D4.

7. Lauren Tarshis, "The Ugly American," *Scholastic Update,* April 3, 1992, p. 2.

8. Lauren Tarshis, "The Voice of the Victim," *Scholastic Update,* April 3, 1992, p. 2.

9. Bob Herbert, "The Prom and the Principal," *The New York Times,* March 16, 1994, p. A21.

Glossary

anti-Semitism—Discrimination against people because they are Jewish.

civil rights—Individual freedoms legally guaranteed to all Americans, regardless of their gender, religion, race, or national origin.

freedom of speech—One of the civil rights that is guaranteed to all Americans by the First Amendment to the United States Constitution.

hate crime—Any violent act that is motivated by hatred toward the victim based on bias against the victim's race, religion, gender, or national origin.

Holocaust—The murder of 11 million people, including 6 million Jews, in Europe during the regime of Hitler and the Nazis. Anti-Semitic hate groups often question whether or not the Holocaust really happened.

Know-Nothing Party—A third party that arose in the 1840s, when thousands of Irish immigrants entered the United States. This party supported nativism and opposed the immigration of anyone who was not white and Protestant.

nativism—The belief that white Protestants from Great Britain are the "true Americans." Nativists oppose most immigration.

neo-Nazi—A person in modern times who adopts the anti-Semitism and symbols of the National Socialist (Nazi) Party of Germany that carried out the Holocaust under Adolf Hitler's orders.

politically correct speech—Language that is intended to be completely neutral and not discriminatory. For example, using the term *physically challenged* to describe people with handicaps is politically correct speech. Hate groups often use terms that are insulting and offensive, and they often view policies mandating politically correct speech as violations of their freedom of speech.

religious prejudice—Discrimination that is based on a person's religious beliefs.

skinheads—Groups of people who shave their heads and favor military boots and Nazi symbols. Usually male and white, skinheads are often violent toward minority groups. Some skinheads, however, are nonviolent and nonracist.

swastika—Symbol of Hitler's Nazi Party that is often used by hate groups. To most people, the swastika represents anti-Semitism.

Three-Fifths Compromise—A decision made by the authors of the United States Constitution to count African-American slaves as three fifths of a person in determining representation in Congress. This is one way white supremacy was written into the Constitution.

Violent Crime Control and Law Enforcement Act of 1994—A federal law stating that sentences for people convicted of hate crimes will be longer than those for people convicted of similar crimes that have no bias motivation.

white supremacy—The belief that members of the white race are superior to members of other races. Most hate groups follow white supremacist beliefs.

Further Reading

Barkun, Michael. *Religion and the Racist Right: The Origins of the Christian Identity Movement*. Chapel Hill: The University of North Carolina Press, 1994.

Bushart, Howard L., John R. Craig, and Myra Barnes. *Soldiers of God: White Supremacists and Their Holy War for America*. New York: Kensington Books, 1998.

Coates, James. *Armed and Dangerous: The Rise of the Survivalist Right*. New York: Hill and Wang, 1987.

Cook, Fred J. *The Ku Klux Klan: America's Recurring Nightmare*. New York: Messner, 1989.

Jacobs, James B., and Kimberly Potter. *Hate Crimes: Criminal Law and Identity Politics*. New York: Oxford University Press, 1998.

Landau, Elaine. *The White Power Movement: America's Racist Hate Groups*. Brookfield, Conn.: Millbrook Press, Inc., 1993.

Levin, Jack, and Jack McDevitt. *Hate Crimes: The Rising Tide of Bigotry and Bloodshed*. New York: Plenum Press, 1993.

Newton, Michael, and Judy Ann. *Racial and Religious Violence in America: A Chronology*. New York: Garland Publishers, 1991.

Terkel, Studs. Race: *How Blacks and Whites Feel About the American Obsession*. New York: New Press, 1993.

Wade, Wyn Craig. *The Fiery Cross: The Ku Klux Klan in America*. New York: Simon & Schuster, 1987.

Weber, Michael. *Causes & Consequences of the African-American Civil Rights Movements*. Orlando, Fla.: Raintree Steck-Vaughn, 1998.

Index